J. J. Brody

THE ANASAZI

ANCIENT INDIAN PEOPLE
OF THE AMERICAN SOUTHWEST

RIZZOLI
NEW YORK

First published in the United States of America in 1990 by
RIZZOLI INTERNATIONAL PUBLICATIONS, INC.
300 Park Avenue South, New York, NY 10010

Copyright © 1990
Editoriale Jaca Book spa, Milan, Italy

Library of Congress Cataloging-in-Publication Data

Brody, J. J.
    The Anasazi / Jerry J. Brody.
        p.   cm.
    Includes bibliographical references.
    ISBN 0-8478-1208-1
    1. Pueblo Indians.   I. Title.
E99.P9B73   1990   90-31691
973'.0497--dc20   CIP

Printed and bound in Italy
by G. Canale & C., Spa, Turin

Table of Contents

Preface

My perspective on the Anasazi is that of an art historian rather than an archaeologist. Thus, my concern is to make sense of their history so that I can make sense of their art. But the Anasazi are an archaeologically known and defined culture who had no written history and it is their tangible remains—what an archaeologist would call their "material culture"—that are the primary documents for our knowledge of them. They are revealed by archaeology rather than by the ordinary means by which we are told history. To further compound the problems of methodology and specialization much of what is classified as their material culture may also legitimately be classified as their art.

It is at that point that my path as an art historian diverges from that of the archaeologist, especially the American archaeologist who is an anthropologist. The archaeologist-anthropologist is first and foremost a social scientist concerned with testing general theories about human behavior. The objects of material culture are bits of data to be organized in order to test hypotheses which may, or may not, have anything to do with history. I am, of course, interested in general theories of human behavior—what human is not?—but as a non-specialist, and those parts of the material record that I classify as art have values and uses that make a study of history central to my work. Which is fair enough, things mean only what people say they mean and data are fair game for any number of disciplinary studies.

George Kubler[1] is not the only art historian who has argued that the history of things—of made objects—is both serial, and open-ended. A form is invented, repeated, modified, enveloped within a sequence, it becomes an element of a series, a serial which we may consider as a single historical fact that is composed of many historical facts. All of these facts, these bits of data which are things made by people can, individually or collectively, be examined for meaning. Think of the ritual architecture of ancient Greece.

But history is open-ended. A sequence ends, yet elements of it may be introduced into alien contexts and reintegrated into other sequences, series, serials. Objects, forms, things can become multiple historical facts as they become integrated into different sequences. And, not only are their possible meanings infinite, but all of them, no matter how contradictory, may be valid and true. Think of nineteenth-century Greek revival architecture. The history of things can be a wondrously complex study, for objects pull us along as they are pushed and pulled through history.

The history of a sequence may be inferred by the forms of which it is composed, and the inferences tested by context—documentation. It is the work of the historian to follow the sequence wherever it may lead. In the case of the Anasazi, it appears that we are given both the things and their contexts by archaeology, which tells us who and what the Anasazi were. But that is not quite the whole story. All students of the Anasazi know that, when we look at the surviving remnants of their world through the filter of Pueblo culture, the sequence never ended. Instead, during the last four-hundred years, after the Anasazi were drawn into the orbit of Euro-American history, it just had a different name. To students interested primarily in how and why the Anasazi initiated the invention of forms, the continuing history of those forms may hold little interest. But a history of the Anasazi is only the first part of a continuing history of a people we call the Pueblo Indians and that is the history that I try to tell here.

I had a great deal of help and wish to give special thanks to Dudley King for many reasons, but most obviously for the use of his photographs, to Melinda Fay for searching out visual materials for me, to Katrina Lasko for her drawings, and to Rodney Hook for his fine artifact pictures. At the Museum of New Mexico Arthur Oliva and Richard Rudisill, Photo Archivists, and Louise Stiver, Collections Manager of the Museum of Indian Art and Culture and the Laboratory of Anthropology were especially helpful. Lynn Brittner and Michael Hering of the Indian Art Research Center, School of American Research (SAR), and Jane Kepp, Deborah Flynn, and David Noble, also of SAR are all thanked for a variety of helpful roles. I owe thanks also to Marian Rodee, Kriztina Kosse, Natalie Pattison, Janet Fragua Hevey, and Kim Trinkaus at the Maxwell Museum of Anthropology, University of New Mexico; and Kim McLean of the National Park Service (former Chaco Center) for many favors. Rebecca Allen and Pamela Hearne were generous to me at the University Museum, University of Pennsylvania and Tom Baker, Don Weaver, Giovanna Belcastro, Alberto Contri, and Nancy Hammack must all be thanked also for pictorial materials. And, finally I thank Sante Bagnoli of Jaca Book whose idea this was, and Caterina Longanesi, editor of this book, who truly facilitated the work.

Chapter One
THE ANASAZI: AN INTRODUCTION

1. The American Southwest.

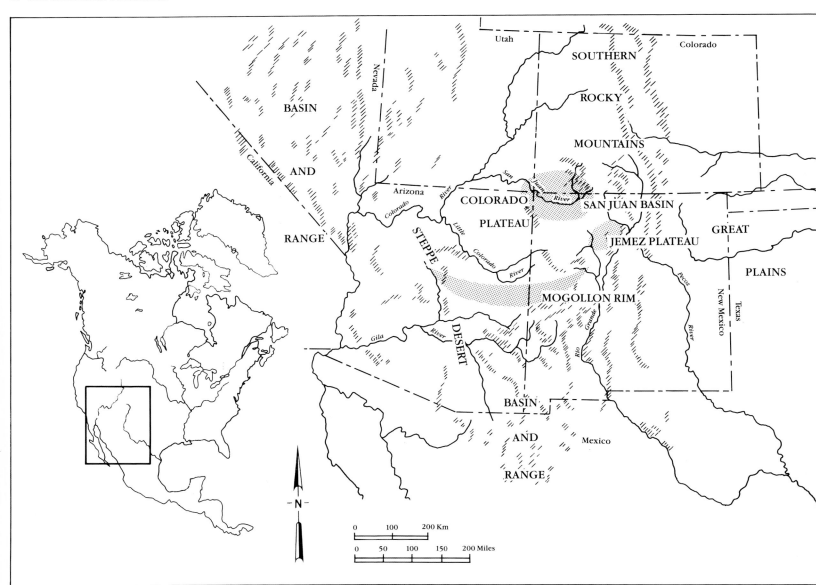

The Anasazi and Their Land

The people whom we call Anasazi once lived in what is now the southwestern United States including New Mexico, Arizona, and parts of Utah and Colorado. The landscape of that vast, arid country is notable for rugged mountain ranges, high plateaus, and many other dramatic geographical features. Only a few rivers drain the region, none of which are navigable. The Rio Grande rises in the Rocky Mountains of southern Colorado and is the longest, flowing for hundreds of miles southward through New Mexico, bending east to form the lengthy border between Texas and Mexico's northeastern frontier, and finally emptying into the Atlantic Ocean through the Gulf of Mexico. Of its major tributaries, only the Pecos is a southwestern river. It flows in a southeasterly direction from its source in the Sangre de Cristo mountains of northeastern New Mexico to join the Rio Grande in west Texas.

Like the Rio Grande, the Colorado River also rises in the southern Rocky Mountains, but it flows southwesterly through Utah and Arizona to empty into the Gulf of California, an arm of the Pacific Ocean sometimes called the Sea of Cortez. Several major streams drain into it in Utah, New Mexico, and Arizona, among them the San Juan and the Little Colorado, whose waters helped create the Grand Canyon in northern Arizona, and the Gila and Salt Rivers which bisect southern Arizona from east to west. The San Juan rises in the southern Rockies, the other three in the mountains of the New Mexico-Arizona border country.

From the point where the Rio Grande turns eastward, it serves as a boundary between nations and something of a barrier between northeastern Mexico and the central and eastern United States. For 700 miles west of the Rio Grande, no such natural border isolates northwestern Mexico from the southwestern United States and the two modern nations are joined rather than separated by the Sonoran Desert. The southwest of the United States is the northwest of Mexico, and the two are divided only by a political history with European origins.

There are mountain ranges throughout the region, some of which are formidable and all of which evidence a complex geology. Most are oriented along north-south axes, thus influencing the flow of streams and of animal and human traffic. Several

2. "The Maze", Colorado River, southeastern Utah.

3. Alamo Canyon, Pajarito Plateau, northern New Mexico.

14

high ranges parallel the Rio Grande along both its banks from Texas to Colorado, restricting east-west traffic to passes between the mountains. Some of these are volcanic, including the Jemez Mountains, with enormous craters and mesa tops of volcanic ash overlying more ancient raised seabeds of sandstone. Others, such as the limestone Sandia and Manzano mountains, are seabeds of greater antiquity upthrust more than 10,000 feet above present-day sea level.

From Mexico northward, much of the border country between Arizona and New Mexico is a vast array of rugged volcanic peaks. Westward, in southern Arizona, the Lower Sonoran Desert, about 3,000 feet above sea level, is relatively flat, with volcanic mountains rising sharply here and there. In north-central Arizona, the sandstones, lava flows, and volcanic peaks of the 6,000-foot-high Colorado Plateau thrust forcefully upward along the Mogollon Rim. Eastward, in New Mexico, the Colorado Plateau merges with the highlands of the Upper Sonoran Desert much less abruptly.

The Colorado Plateau, which extends from central New Mexico westward to Nevada, and from the Mogollon Rim northward to the Rockies, was the original Anasazi homeland. Near its center, where nineteenth-century mapmakers created the political boundary that we call the Four Corners, lay the very heart of the Anasazi country. The eastern half of that region, drained by the San Juan River and its tributaries, is known as the San Juan Basin. High, flat-topped mesas, deep

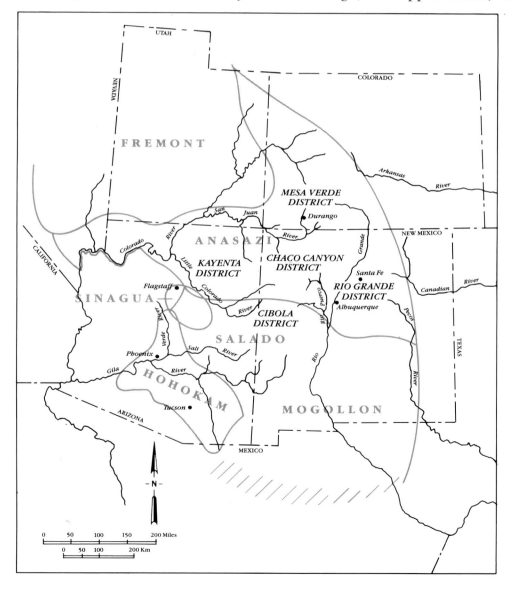

4. Ancient Cultures of the Southwest.

15

canyons, fantastically eroded and brilliantly colored sandstone cliffs, dark volcanic formations, hot summers, cold winters, a monsoon climate, lengthy droughts, late summer thunderstorms, and the resulting, devastating flash floods are all characteristics of this dramatic land.

There is great ecological variation depending on elevation, soil, geology, prevailing winds, and many other environmental factors, and vastly different lifezones may coexist within a few miles of each other. A green oasis may cut across a desert following the flow of a river, and it may even continue for great distances after the river has sunk below the desert floor. Snow may be visible on mountain peaks only a few hours' walk from a searing desert plain. Thunderstorms may be seen all around, yet no rain will fall in one place for months on end. And a dry arroyo in a dry landscape may flood suddenly, wildly, filled with water that was deposited far upstream by a distant cloudburst.

5. The Anasazi World at the time of European contact; still extant Pueblos are in black.

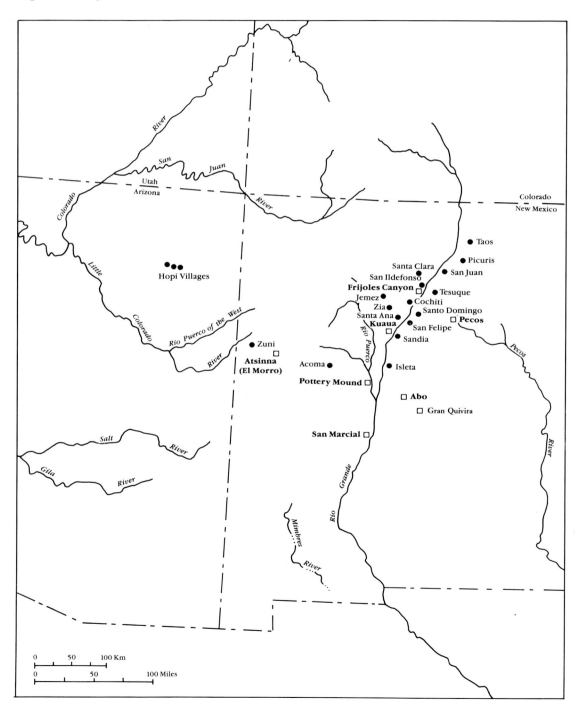

Opposite:

1. Natural Bridges National Park, southeastern Utah.

Following pages:

2. Natural Bridges National Park.

3. Canyon de Chelly, northeastern Arizona.

4. The Grand Canyon from
Indian Gardens overlook,
northern Arizona.

5.6. The Grand
Canyon's South Rim and
the Colorado River.

9. *Axes of fibrolite stone, a maul, bone and antler awls, pins, and a flute. The very hard and beautifully textured fibrolite axes were made in and near Pecos Pueblo and were widely traded. Longest object, 10". Pueblo IV period. Maxwell Museum of Anthropology, Albuquerque.*

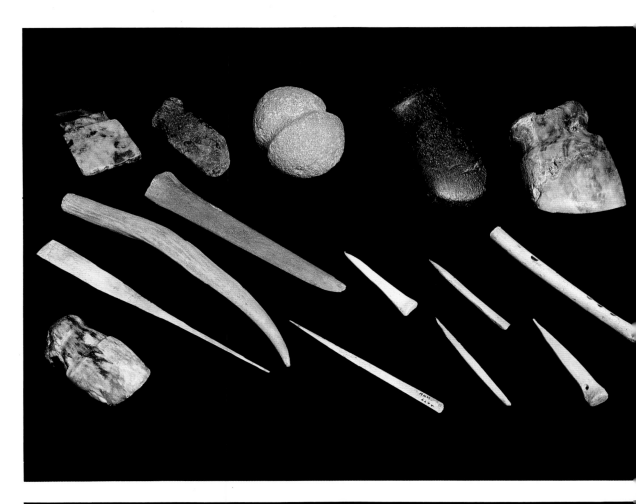

10. *Objects from the site of San Gabriel at San Juan Pueblo, New Mexico, the first Spanish settlement in the southwest, 1598-1607. There are two brass candlestick bases, the largest about 2 ¹/₂" high, rusted chain mail, Mexican majolica pottery fragments, and a Flemish carved bone ornament from the stock of a firearm. Maxwell Museum of Anthropology, Albuquerque.*

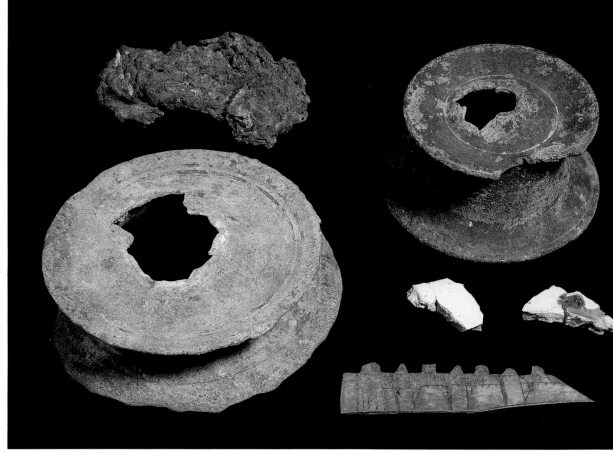

11. Top row: Hohokam ax, Classic period; Anasazi ax of limonite, Pueblo IV; Anasazi arrowshaft straightener, Pueblo IV. From top down: wooden throwing stick for hunting small game, Archaic era; wooden spear foreshaft with stone point, late Archaic or early Basket Maker; wooden "atlatl" (spearthrower), Paleo-Indian or early Archaic; stone knife in wooden haft, Pueblo III (replica); reed arrow with hardwood point, Pueblo II. Atlatl is 33" long. All wooden objects from southern New Mexico. Maxwell Museum of Anthropology, Albuquerque.

12. Painted wooden fragments, probably of an altar construction. Birds which carry prayers to the sky and dragonflies, frogs, and other animals associated with water were all important in Anasazi art. Largest fragment is 3" long. Cibola district, New Mexico. ca. 1300. Maxwell Museum of Anthropology, Albuquerque.

13. *Anasazi shell pendants from the Pacific Ocean and the Gulf of Mexico, largest is 3" long. Pueblo IV, Rio Grande drainage. Laboratory of Anthropology, Museum of New Mexico, Santa Fe.*

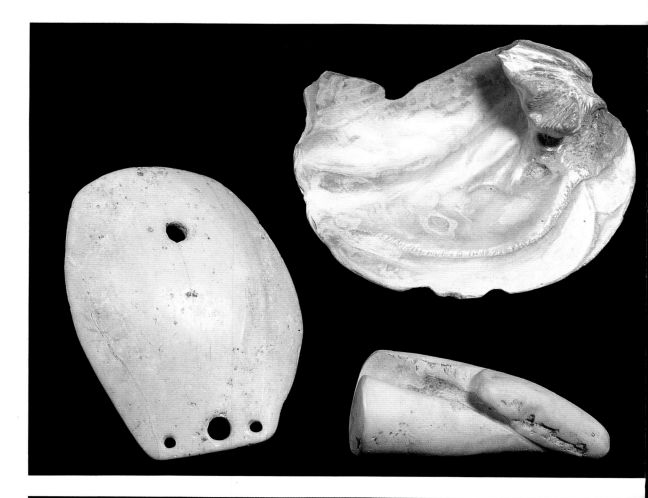

14. *Paleo-Indian spear points. From top left: Folsom, Folsom, Firstview, Sandia; second row: Clovis, Clovis, Ventana complex, Ventana complex. Longest is 3". Maxwell Museum of Anthropology, Albuquerque.*

15. Stone hoe, wooden scoop, and Anasazi foods—maize, beans, squash, sunflower seeds, and prickly pear cactus, all recovered from eleventh-century sites in Chaco Canyon, New Mexico. Scoop is 18" long. National Park Service and Maxwell Museum of Anthropology, Albuquerque.

16. Archaic, Hopewell, and early Woodland stone objects from the Ohio Valley, eastern United States. The bird like figures (about 5" long) are "atlatl" weights dating to about 3000 B.C. Great care was taken in the selection of materials as well as careful workmanship. Maxwell Museum of Anthropology, Albuquerque.

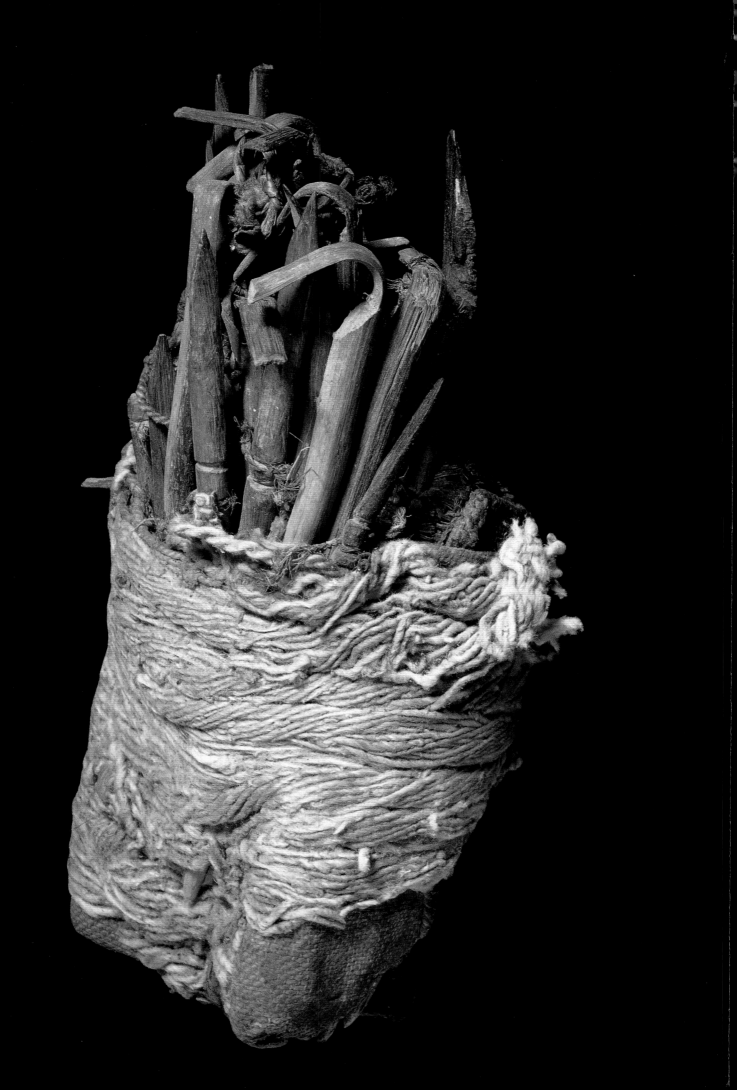

Because of the ecological variety, this hard land is rich in natural food resources. People have lived here for thousands of years, hunting, gathering wild plants and, for the past 3,000 years or more, planting gardens of domesticated crops. Among the wild plants that thrive in one life zone or another are agave, cacti, mesquite, amaranth, piñon, grapes, hackberry, walnuts, yucca, and many others whose fruit, seeds, leaves, bark and roots were—and still are—used by native people of the region for food, or medicine, or to be processed and made into tools or other useful products. The animal life is as varied; deer, antelope, and rabbits are locally plentiful and were important sources of animal protein and raw materials such as sinew and hides. Larger animals such as elk and bison were also hunted, as were the many smaller creatures of the different lifezones including rodents, reptiles, and insects.

The Anasazi way of life was created amid these environments. First emerging as a distinct group less than 2,000 years ago, the Anasazi were neither the only village-dwelling farmers of the region, nor the earliest, but they flourished, ultimately to become the largest and best known of all prehistoric southwestern cultures. We do not know what they called themselves and must doubt that they even identified themselves as a single society. They were never politically unified, spoke at least six mutually unintelligible languages,[1] and it is unlikely that they were ethnically homogeneous. Their name comes from an English language corruption of a Navajo Indian word for the many abandoned stone ruins of the Four Corners. It is a matter of debate whether the original Navajo term meant "the ancient ones" or "enemies of our ancient ones;" in either case, the word *Anasazi* was never used by the people now called by that name. It may best be understood as the name we now give to a successful way of life that was shared by many different peoples.

The ruins of Anasazi towns are found throughout their ancient homeland, and archaeologists recognize several regional centers. Important among these are the Rio Grande valley and Chaco Canyon in New Mexico, the Cibola-Little Colorado area of New Mexico and Arizona, the Mesa Verde district of Colorado and Utah, and the Kayenta region of Arizona. The many modern-day Pueblo Indian tribes living along the southern, eastern, and western margins of the Colorado Plateau are descendents of the Anasazi; the Navajo, who gave them their name, are not.

Methodology: What We Know and How We Know It

The Anasazi, in common with most native peoples of North America, had no written history and, in that sense, were truly prehistoric. Therefore, our knowledge of them is largely inferential and comes from three primary sources. First, there are the tangible archaeological remains of their civilization, second, the written records of sixteenth-century Spanish explorers who had contact with them, and third, the traditions of their Pueblo Indian descendants.

There are many thousands of Anasazi archaeological sites, ranging from campsites that might have been used by a single person for only one night, to stone and adobe communities with hundreds of rooms that were continuously occupied for centuries. Most sites fall between these extremes, containing several buildings with a few dozen rooms that were lived in for only one or two generations.

The surviving objects from these places are typically made of stone, pottery, shell, or bone. Exotic materials from distant regions are often found, and human skeletal remains are not uncommon. Where the combination of aridity and cultural habits allowed, perishable and fibrous materials such as woven textiles, cordage, basketry, wood, leather, and even foodstuffs have survived to the present day.

The archaeological record provides us with considerable demographic

Opposite:

17. Anasazi basketry container with carved and painted wooden prayer sticks made as shrine offerings. Container wrapped with woven cloth and cotton yarn, 11" long. Pueblo II period, north-central New Mexico. Maxwell Museum of Anthropology, Albuquerque.

information about the Anasazi, giving a fair idea of their physical attributes, lifespan, diet, and health. We are well-informed about manufacturing technologies and, to a lesser degree, about the economic, social, and religious activities surrounding the use or the creation of Anasazi artifacts. Finally, archaeological objects provide many clues about the culture of the Anasazi, giving us some notion about their philosophical, religious, and aesthetic values and systems.

The Anasazi historical record begins in the sixteenth century when the Hispanic conquerors of Mexico first made contact with them. By the 1530s the Spanish had become aware of an isolated group of town-dwelling farmers who wore woven cotton clothing—and therefore were civilized by their reckoning—living on the northernmost frontier of Mexico. From 1540 to 1542 a large expedition, under the leadership of Francisco Vasquez de Coronado, was licensed by the Spanish government to explore Anasazi territory. The chronicles and letters written by members of that force are the oldest eyewitness descriptions that we have of the Anasazi world, an invaluable historical resource which allows us to refine our interpretations of archaeological materials and to bridge the era between prehistory and history.

During the fifty years following Coronado's expedition, Anasazi country was visited officially and unofficially by several smaller Spanish forces, most of whom left a legacy of chronicles, letters, and even legal depositions describing aspects of Anasazi life and culture. A few Catholic priests and Mexican Indian auxiliaries were sometimes left behind when their companions withdrew, but their impact was relatively minor and these alien residents left no known accounts of their adventures. It appears that the Mexican Indians were generally absorbed by the Anasazi, while the priests rarely survived for more than a few months. It was not until 1598 that a sanctioned Hispanic colonizing expedition was sent to Anasazi country under the leadership of Don Juan de Oñate. The Oñate expedition to the Rio Grande Valley marks both the beginning of a permanent European presence in the Southwest and the end of the Anasazi era.

The Hispanic explorers called the Anasazi people *Pueblos*, meaning town dwellers, to distinguish them from other native peoples of the northern Mexican frontier, whom they considered to be uncivilized. The name *Pueblo* became

6. Fifteenth-century mural, Kiva 9, Pottery Mound, Rio Grande district, New Mexico. (Reconstruction by Paul Kay.) Original painting was about 48″ high. The horned and feathered serpent is associated with water and is still an important personage in Pueblo ritual dramas. It seems to have entered the Anasazi world from Mexico at about the same time as the Kachina Societies. Maxwell Museum of Anthropology, Albuquerque.

established, and is still used by about nineteen present-day tribes when they refer to themselves collectively, as well as by most other people. In many respects the Pueblo groups are similar, and their descent from the Anasazi is apparent, so that interpretation of Anasazi lifeways by analogy with documented Pueblo customs has a certain validity. But the Pueblo tribes are, in fact, separate peoples, each distinct from all others, suggesting yet another analogy: like the Pueblos, the Anasazi were a corporate people only when compared to their neighbors, but that collective was made up of many distinct communities.

Curiosity about the Anasazi seems to have been dormant for centuries. The Pueblos and other local tribes knew in a general way—and sometimes quite specifically—who had lived in the long-abandoned ruins of the Colorado Plateau. They preserved traditions about the Anasazi during more than two centuries of Spanish rule and a half century of control by an independent Mexican nation. But the Southwest was poverty ridden during most of that time, and both Indian and Hispanic townspeople and farmers suffered terribly from epidemic diseases and were often threatened by mobile, raiding Indian neighbors, who now occupied much of the ancient Anasazi homeland. Peace, economic security, political stability, and wealth were necessary before scholarly interest in the Anasazi could develop. Those conditions were not met until after the middle of the nineteenth century when, following the 1846 war between Mexico and the United States, the Southwest was ceded to the United States.

It was only through that political accident that Anasazi studies became an Anglo-American rather than a Mexican enterprise, with both theory and method peculiarly American. The Southwest came to be used as a major field laboratory wherein American archaeology and ethnology evolved.[2] In the absence of written history,

7. Richard Wetherill (center) excavating an Anasazi burial, probably at Chaco Canyon. Photographer unknown, ca. 1896. Museum of New Mexico, Santa Fe. Wetherill and his brothers were ranchers in Colorado who opened up exploration of the Mesa Verde ruins in the 1880s. Richard later explored Anasazi ruins throughout the Southwest and with George Pepper excavated at Pueblo Bonito for the American Museum of Natural History.

archaeology became an anthropological discipline rather than an historical one. Its expressed concern was with "the ethnology of the past" rather than with historical reconstruction, and the pueblos and Pueblo Indians came to be used more for ethnological than for historical research. From an archaeological perspective, Pueblo behavior was to be studied so that the Anasazi sociocultural system might be better understood. Meanwhile, the Anasazi's descendants were sometimes involved, sometimes ignored, sometimes bemused, and often exploited observers of the alien people who were studying their ancestors.

Time and Space of Anasazi Culture History

Although anthropological perspectives rather than historical ones dominated Anasazi scholarship for many years, a considerable amount of historical reconstruction was done. A broad outline of Anasazi culture history emerged, with general agreement among scholars about most historical issues, despite significant

	PECOS CLASSIFICATION	ROBERTS CLASSIFICATION	RIO GRANDE SEQUENCE (After Wendorf and Reed)
2000 1900 1800 1700	PUEBLO V	HISTORIC PUEBLO	HISTORIC
1600 1500 1400	PUEBLO IV	REGRESSIVE PUEBLO	CLASSIC
1300 1200	PUEBLO III	GREAT PUEBLO	COALITION
1100 1000 900	PUEBLO II	DEVELOPMENTAL PUEBLO	DEVELOPMENTAL
800 700	PUEBLO I		
600 500	BASKET MAKER III	MODIFIED BASKET MAKER	
400 300 200 100	BASKET MAKER II	BASKET MAKER	PRE-CERAMIC
AD BC 100 200 300	BASKET MAKER I (Hypothetical) ?	?	?

8. Alternative syntheses of Anasazi-Pueblo Culture History.

areas of interpretive disagreement.[3] Many details of Anasazi culture history remain unresolved, and no single summary outline of history is accurate for all Anasazi regions for all times. Dates for cultural stages and phases differ from place to place, not all occur in all places, and attributes of different phases vary considerably between regions. For those reasons, a synthesis of several culture history models is used here.

Euro-American rather than Native American spatial, temporal, and historical concepts dominate all orthodox reconstructions. Pueblo traditional histories, which are certainly stylized in non-European modes, rarely conform well with scholarly historical objectives and, therefore, are generally ignored, or treated metaphorically or as fiction. Scholarly syntheses of Anasazi culture history tend to have an evolutionary bias and a materialist perspective, and are designed to explain known or presumed archaeological facts. These reconstructions have changed over the decades in response to new information and to new theoretical concepts about human behavior, but their basic premises are little different today than they were a century ago. In general, Anasazi culture is assumed to have become more complex with the passage of time, and cultural decisions by Anasazi people are explained as though motivated primarily by the desire to increase economic and social efficiency. The latter assumption is in opposition to dominant themes of traditional Pueblo histories, which tell of the emergence of a people and their consequent efforts to live in balanced harmony with the entire universe.

Mid-nineteenth-century investigators often interpreted Anasazi culture as a colonial or provincial offshoot of the Toltec or Aztec cultures of ancient Mexico. Some even denied historical connection between Anasazi and Pueblo peoples. By the end of the century, field work at large Anasazi sites, archaeological surveys, and awareness of sixteenth-century Hispanic chronicles had all demonstrated the accuracy of native traditions. The Anasazi were now accepted as the ancestors of

	ANASAZI	HOHOKAM	MOGOLLON	MIMBRES MOGOLLON	CASAS GRANDES	SINAGUA	FREMONT (Great Salt Lake District, only)
1900	(Modern)	(Modern)					
1800	PUEBLO V	PIMA-PAPAGO	?	?			
1700					?	?	?
1600		PROTO-HISTORIC					
1500	PUEBLO IV		? SALADO?	? SALADO?			
1400						CLEAR CREEK	
1300	PUEBLO III	CLASSIC	MOGOLLON 5	ANIMAS PHASE		TURKEY HILL	LEVEE PHASE
1200				?	MEDIO PERIOD	ELDEN FOCUS	
1100						WINONA PHASE	
1000	PUEBLO II	SEDENTARY	MOGOLLON 4	CLASSIC MIMBRES		RIO DE FLAG	
900			MOGOLLON 3	THREE CIRCLE PHASE	VIEJO PERIOD		
800	PUEBLO I	COLONIAL	MOGOLLON 2	SAN FRANCISCO PHASE		SUNSET	BEAR RIVER PHASE
700				GEORGE-TOWN PHASE		CINDER PARK	
600	BASKET MAKER III						
500							
400	BASKET MAKER II	PIONEER	MOGOLLON 1	EARLY PIT HOUSE PERIOD	PLAINWARE PERIOD		
300						?	?
200							
100	?						
AD / BC		?	?	?	?		

DESERT ARCHAIC TRADITIONS

9. Major Prehistoric Cultures of the Southwest.

37

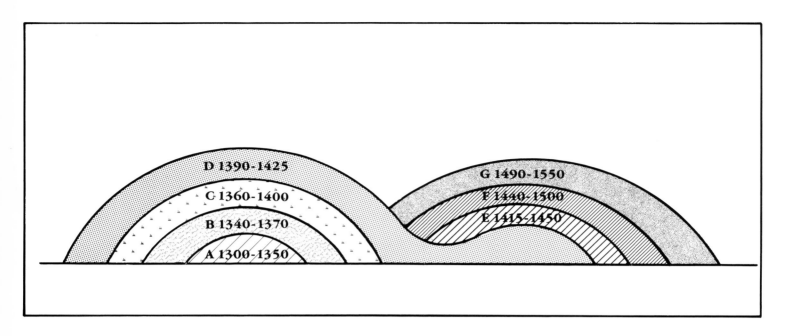

10. Stratigraphy and seriation. Stratigraphy is established when deposits are made sequentially. Stratum D links the two mounds for it is at the top of one and at the bottom of the other. Recognition of such overlapping (called seriation) is a major tool of Southwestern archaeologists. Style differences between materials (such as pottery) which are sequentially deposited in a site may be compared from site to site thus relating them historically and temporally. (Adapted from Kidder: 1962.)

modern Pueblo tribes, but complexity at Anasazi sites was still interpreted as being due to responses to the diffusion of ideas, technology, and even people from ancient Mexico.[4] Except that they were surely prehistoric and presumably contemporaneous with Toltec or Aztec cultures, there was no consensus about Anasazi antiquity.

During the first half of the twentieth century, a great many field surveys and excavations provided evidence for the slow evolution of Anasazi culture within the Southwest. Contacts with Mexico were undeniable, but the perception of Anasazi culture as a provincial outpost of Mexican culture was no longer attractive. Investigations in other parts of the Southwest broadened understanding of the variability of ancient cultures of the region, and the Anasazi were now perceived as only one of several contemporaneous, town-dwelling, farming peoples of the region. A variety of new archaeological techniques were invented and refined in these years. Relative chronologies, both within and between sites, were established through seriation and ceramic analysis and, by mid-century absolute dating was made possible by use of tree ring analysis, radiocarbon methods, and other objective means.

After about 1950, many other analytical procedures came into common use as thousands of ancient Southwestern sites were investigated. Anthropological orientations dominated and, for several decades, analyses were directed toward reconstructing social mechanisms at particular sites rather than toward the history of those places or their relationships to other communities. In recent years, research interests have shifted to focus on community interactions within relatively large geographical and ecological zones such as canyons, mesas, river drainage systems, and even such complex geographical entities as the San Juan Basin. As yet, there is little renewed interest in recreating Anasazi culture history beyond the needs of research programs that are primarily concerned with issues of human ecology.

Paleo-Indian and Archaic Ancestors

No humans that we know of lived in the Southwest before the very end of the last geological epoch that we call the "Pleistocene" or "Ice Age." During that comparatively wet and cool period there were a few isolated glaciers on high mountain ranges within the region and many large and small lakes in basin areas that today are often treeless, alkaline deserts. Between about 10,000 and 15,000 years ago, different groups of people, whom we call Paleo-Indians, hunted now extinct species of elephant, bison, camel, and horse that roamed the rich grasslands of the area. We know these people best by their beautifully crafted spear points and other stone tools which are our primary means for differentiating among them. Many of these implements resemble contemporaneous tools found elsewhere in the New World, suggesting that the earliest southwestern people participated in cultural traditions that were very widespread.

Though stone-hunting, hide-working, and butchering tools comprise the vast majority of surviving artifacts of these ancient people, there is some evidence that they built shelters of brush or skins, made a variety of bone tools, and sewed tailored skin clothing. It is likely that they boiled water for cooking by dropping hot stones into water-filled skin vessels, and they made other skin and basketry containers, nets, animal decoys, wooden tools—including spear throwers (*atlatls*)—and ornaments. Their only art that seems to have survived are a few fragmentary pieces of engraved bone.

They apparently organized themselves into relatively small groups or bands, which regularly moved from one hunting or food-gathering location to another, using and reusing the same campsites over the course of many generations. Their hunting methods were diverse, including such strategies as stampeding herds of bison over a cliff, or trapping elephants and other large game animals in boggy meadows where they could easily be speared. We know very little of their other economic activities, but may reasonably assume that they also hunted and trapped small animals and gathered useful wild plants that were plentiful in that ancient environment. We know also that some flintlike cherts, obsidian, and other desirable stones were quarried and then traded as raw materials over great distances.

The transition toward a warm, dry climate much like that of the present-day Southwest caused dramatic changes in animal and plant populations. It began about 9,000 years ago and was substantially completed 1,500 years later. We do not know

11. A spear or javelin thrown with the aid of an *atlatl* will go further and more accurately than if thrown by hand.

12. Split twig animal figurines, Grand Canyon, Arizona. Archaic era. Thought to have been religious offerings. Ht. 5″. School of American Research.

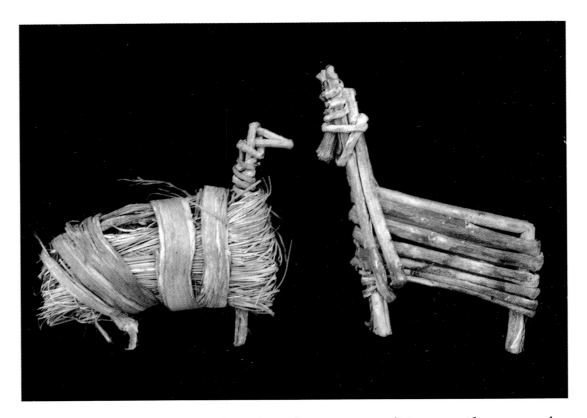

which Paleo-Indian groups adapted to these new conditions, or if new peoples migrated to the region, but, in any case, people we variously call Desert Culture, Desert Archaic, or Archaic, thrived in the Southwest as they did in neighboring parts of North America. The Desert Archaic people relied for sustenance on harvesting a broad spectrum of wild plants and hunted and trapped small and large animals. Their populations grew, and their manufacturing technologies became more complex, as evidenced by the great variety of cultural artifacts recovered from dry caves throughout western North America which testify to their skill in textile, basketry, and woodworking arts. Curiously, Archaic era stone tools, which now included milling implements used to grind plant foods into flour, are considerably less elegant than those of earlier times.

Many impressive Archaic era paintings and engravings have been preserved on cliff walls and in caves throughout the Southwest and neighboring regions. Some are of animal subjects and describe hunting activities, and others seem to picture religious rituals and complex symbolizing systems that very generally resemble certain modern-day tribal religions, classified as shamanic. In other respects as well, there is good evidence to show increased social complexity during these centuries.

The gradual population increase and the growth of social and technological complexity were paralleled by an apparent broadening of hunting and food-gathering activities and the development of regional traditions, each marked by a distinctive assemblage of stone tools. As much as anything, these variations seem to have been responses to the various local ecosystems that were a consequence of the progressive dessication of the landscape. By about 5500 B.C., two distinct Archaic traditions had evolved within the Southwest: the Cochise Culture, found south of the Mogollon Rim, and the Oshara Culture, found to the north and east of the Cochise on the Colorado Plateau. By about 2000 B.C., people of both the Cochise and Oshara traditions were gardening by nurturing wild plants, even building crude water control systems for them. During the succeeding millennium, maize was acquired, and the transition to an agricultural way of life was well under way. The Anasazi were among the descendants of these ancient Desert Archaic people.

The era of the Anasazi began about 2,000 years ago, seemingly originating on the Colorado Plateau, but owing much to the experiences of people living south of their homeland. The subsistence base for their sedentary lifeway was horticulture, learned from neighbors, dependent upon plants originating in Mexico, and importantly supplemented by hunting and foraging. Interactions amongst all early farming peoples of the Southwest were continual, and Anasazi history, for all its unique qualities, is inseparable from that of its neighbors, some of whom ultimately merged with the Anasazi. Relationships with more distant peoples, especially of Middle America and even of eastern North America are less clear, but must also be considered if we are to understand Anasazi history.

The ancestors of the Anasazi had been a Desert Archaic people but, unlike some nearby Desert Archaic folk, who maintained fundamentally conservative economic and social systems until very recent times, the Anasazi changed radically. As time passed, their culture became increasingly complex and drifted ever further from its Archaic origins and from that of peoples with whom they had once shared virtual cultural identity. Even so, the archaeological record demonstrates many contacts in prehistoric times between the Anasazi and their hunter-gatherer neighbors.

Far to the east, between the Mississippi Valley and the Atlantic Ocean, other native North Americans created complex societies that were even more ancient and, in some ways, more spectacular than those of the Southwest. Despite many

	ANASAZI	CENTRAL MEXICO	MAYA		OAXACA	EASTERN NORTH AMERICA	
1600	HISTORIC ERA	SPANISH CONQUEST	SPANISH CONQUEST		SPANISH CONQUEST	/////////	/////
1500	PUEBLO IV	AZTEC (Late Post-Classic)	LATE POST-CLASSIC	LATE	MONTE ALBAN V	LATE MISSISSIPPIAN	
1400							
1300	/////////				/////////	/////////	LATE WOODLAND
1200	PUEBLO III	/////////	/////////			MISSISSIPPIAN	
1100	/////////	TOLTEC (Post-Classic)	EARLY POST-CLASSIC		MONTE ALBAN IV	/////////	
1000	PUEBLO II		/////////			EARLY MISSISSIPPIAN	
900	/////////		TERMINAL CLASSIC			/////////	
800	PUEBLO I	/////////	/////////			SOUTHERN HOPEWELL	
700	/////////	TEOTIHUACAN IV (Late Classic)	(LATE)		/////////		
600	BASKET MAKER III	/////////			MONTE ALBAN III B	/////////	/////
500			CLASSIC	MIDDLE			
400	/////////	TEOTIHUACAN III (Classic)			/////////		MIDDLE WOODLAND
300	BASKET MAKER II		(EARLY)		MONTE ALBAN III A	OHIO HOPEWELL	
200	/////////	/////////	/////////		/////////		
100							
AD BC	(ARCHAIC)	TEOTIHUACAN II (Proto-Classic)	LATE PRE-CLASSIC		MONTE ALBAN II	/////////	
100	∿						
200		/////////			/////////		/////
300		TEOTIHUACAN I (Pre-Classic)	/////////			ADENA	EARLY WOODLAND
400			MIDDLE PRE-CLASSIC	EARLY	MONTE ALBAN I	∿	∿

13. Anasazi cultural sequences compared to other regions of pre-Columbian America.

41

similarities between the two regions, especially in the realms of food production, art, and ritual, there is relatively little physical evidence of direct contacts between them in prehistoric times. For that reason, and because so many of the shared attributes suggest derivation from ancient Middle America, it is likely that each region responded to some form of independent contact with Mexican cultures.

Nonetheless, the evidence of ancient contacts between eastern North America and the Southwest is intriguing. In 1540, when Francisco Vasquez de Coronado first met the Anasazi at Zuni Pueblo, a trading party from Pecos Pueblo came to Zuni.[5] A member of that group seems to have been a Plains Indian, who told the Spanish of a great river that was almost certainly the Mississippi, and described Mississippian civilization to them, stimulating their interest in exploration eastward. Even before Europeans reintroduced horses to North America, thus revolutionizing hunting and transportation across the Great Plains, the bison herds of that region had regularly been hunted by both the eastern Anasazi and the westernmost of the Mississippian people. Hunting parties from the two regions apparently met on occasion, and their trading parties also crossed the Plains. Farming villages of the expanding eastern cultures were located along the river systems that fed the Mississippi from the Rocky Mountains, and there were contacts between those communities and the eastern Anasazi. Thus, for all its barren vastness, the Great Plains had been a point of limited contact between the two North American civilizations, each of which was also separately influenced in many different ways from Middle America.

There is a vast body of evidence for direct and indirect contacts between the Southwest and Mexico.[6] The Sonoran Desert extends a thousand miles southward from the Colorado Plateau to central Mexico, and Paleo-Indian and Archaic peoples of that entire region shared one land and its resources. Maize was first domesticated by Archaic people in the arid highlands of the Upper Sonoran Desert of central Mexico in about 6500 B.C., and its use spread from there in all directions. Maize, beans, and squash, the domesticated plants that were fundamental to village life in the Southwest, as well as to many other American societies, all came from Mexico. Anasazi civilization was made possible by that sacred triad and, as time passed, many other kinds of knowledge critical to the character and quality of Anasazi life also came from the south. Cotton, loom weaving, pottery technology, irrigation and other agricultural techniques, the bow-and-arrow, sea shells used for ornaments, macaws and copper bells used in ritual, and all sorts of sacred knowledge all came to the Anasazi by way of northern, western, and central Mexico.

Other than the certainty that relationships with the south were dynamic, we know very little about the mechanisms. Trade relationships were widespread and by no means one-sided; Anasazi turquoise and other raw materials and manufactures were highly valued in Mexico and Middle America. The Anasazi gathered seashells from the Gulf of California and the shores of the Pacific Ocean, and some went even further afield. We know that there were Anasazi who spoke Nahuatl, the language of the Valley of Mexico in the sixteenth century, and that Anasazi textiles were valued in Sonora, 400 miles south of the Four Corners. From the eleventh to the fourteenth centuries, the Anasazi traded at Casas Grandes in Chihuahua, hundreds of miles south of the Colorado Plateau, a town with political, ritual, and economic ties to the Toltec cities of the Valley of Mexico. Even after the downfall of the Toltecs, trade with the south continued.

There were political and religious ramifications to these relationships. The great city-states of the Valley of Mexico and Middle America were vastly more complex and expansive than were the Anasazi or any other North American culture. Their energy reached far afield, strongly influencing the somewhat less elaborate societies of northwestern Mexico such as the Guasave and Chalchihuites who, in turn, may

14. Copper bells made in western Mexico are probably the most common Mexican trade objects found in the Southwest. These are from New Mexico, Pueblo II, ca. 1000. Largest about 1″ long. Laboratory of Anthropology, Museum of New Mexico, Santa Fe.

have provided the most regular contacts between the Anasazi and Middle American civilizations. In light of all this, interpreting smaller societies such as the Anasazi as provincial, marginal or even impoverished versions of the complex cultures of the south, seems reasonable. But the Anasazi were more than "unfinished" Middle Americans. They knew who they were and pragmatically selected from amongst many possibilities only those things from Middle America that they considered useful. And, virtually everything that was alien, but accepted, was modified, reshaped to fit a pattern that was comfortable to them.

Anasazi Neighbors of the American Southwest

Other than the Anasazi, the best known prehistoric farmers of the Southwest were two groups descended from the Cochise Branch of the Desert Archaic whom we now call the Hohokam and the Mogollon. The former lived in the low deserts of south-central Arizona and in the central Arizona highlands. The far more heterogenous Mogollon people lived in the mountainous border country between Arizona and New Mexico, in the southeastern deserts of New Mexico, and in the Lower Sonoran Desert of northern Mexico. Many other prehistoric sedentary groups are described in the archaeological literature, some visible in the archaeological record for only a few generations, others known for longer time periods, but from relatively small and isolated regions. Among such groups whose histories intersected with the Anasazi in significant ways are the Salado, the Fremont, and the Sinagua. All lived in places that bordered the Anasazi on one hand, and the Mogollon or Hohokam on the other.

The best known Hohokam community is a large and complicated site called Snaketown, located between the modern cities of Phoenix and Tucson in Arizona. Snaketown was occupied from perhaps 300 B.C. to about A.D. 1300. Excavations there during the 1930s and the 1960s document Hohokam culture history, which is divided into several distinct periods.[7] There is debate about the beginning of the Hohokam era, some archaeologists arguing that its Pioneer period began as early as 300 B.C., others dating its origins as recently as A.D. 500. A beginning date of about A.D. 200 to 300 may be most reasonable.[8]

Pioneer period people lived in small, scattered villages of wattle and daub houses. They built many miles of irrigation canals to draw water for their fields from the Gila and Salt rivers, which flow through their low desert country. Among their many household arts were weaving, which made use of wild vegetable fibers, pottery making, and fashioning shell jewelry. Their ritual arts included the manufacture of small human and animal pottery figurines, probably used in agricultural rites, and stone effigy vessels, perhaps used as incense burners. These objects, the elaborate canal systems, and other material remains seem to support the proposition that the earliest Hohokam people had actually emigrated northward from western Mexico.

During the Colonial period, Hohokam populations increased, new communities were established in the mountains and plateaus of central and eastern Arizona, and their social and ritual systems became increasingly complex. Virtually all Pioneer period crafts were elaborated upon both technically and stylistically, and Colonial era arts are notable for their lively innovations upon traditional themes. The shell trade increased and, when cotton was introduced, it too became an important commodity, either woven or raw, in trade with other southwestern people. Their dead were cremated and their ashes placed in pottery urns and interred in burial fields. Novel Mexican influences are visible in public architecture such as ritual ball courts and truncated pyramids. Copper bells, macaws, and pyrite mirrors were imported from western Mexico.

Communities became larger, but Hohokam territory shrank during the Sedentary and Classic periods as people withdrew to the low-lying desert country that had been their original homeland. The remarkable stylistic and technological continuity of earlier periods continued through Sedentary times but weakened in the Classic period. Classic period towns, such as Casa Grande in south-central Arizona, had large, thick-walled, multistoried adobe houses and were enclosed by high walls. It is thought that the less well-understood Salado Culture of western New Mexico and eastern Arizona exerted a strong influence upon Classic period Hohokam people. In general, there is little direct evidence of interactions between the Hohokam and the Anasazi, but mutual indirect influences may be inferred for all periods.

By the sixteenth century, when the first Europeans came to Arizona, all Hohokam towns were abandoned and Indian people of the Papago and Pima tribes occupied the former Hohokam region. Though they lived materially simple lives in small, isolated *rancherias* and depended on a mixed economy that combined hunting, gathering, and gardening, it is generally believed that these modern people are descendants of the Hohokam.

The Mogollon people are characterized by great variety in material remains and life styles, seemingly due to the many different environments in which they lived. At least six major Mogollon subgroups (called Branches) have been described, each with its own culture history sequence. Most of the groups appear to have been more dependent upon hunting and wild-food gathering than were most other southwestern farmers, and their villages tended to be small, scattered, and composed of deeply excavated houses called pit houses. In most places, their pottery was unpainted brown- or redware. They seem to have had a profound influence upon the earliest Anasazi, whose material remains are sometimes almost identical with those of one or another Mogollon group. In later times, radical changes in

Mogollon house style, community planning, ritual, art styles, and other lifeways reflect heavy influence from the Anasazi.

Perhaps the best known of the Mogollon subgroups is the Mimbres Branch of southwestern New Mexico. Mimbres artists of their Classic period (ca. A.D. 1000-1150) made remarkable black-and-white painted pottery often used as mortuary offerings. Mimbres burial customs and the subject matter of some of their pottery paintings and rock art suggest north Mexican practices, but their pottery technology and painting style was certainly influenced by the Anasazi.

Most Mogollon villages were abandoned and the people scattered during the century following A.D. 1150. A similar phenomenon occurred in many other parts of the Southwest between the twelfth and fourteenth centuries, and it is likely that groups such as the Salado were descended from among these dispersed peoples. It is not known which modern Indian tribes are descended from the Mogollon, but many Mogollon people certainly joined with Anasazi groups whose descendants are the Pueblo tribes of Arizona and New Mexico.

Anasazi Descendants: the Pueblo[9] People

There are about nineteen Pueblo Indian tribes today with a total population of about 50,000. They are modern people, who have successfully preserved their Anasazi-derived values and social and religious institutions, despite more than 400 years of European political domination. Descendents of other ancient Southwestern peoples who were sometimes bitter enemies of the Anasazi and their Pueblo descendants also continue to live in the region and are equally independent.

When Coronado came to the Southwest,[10] he found that most of the pueblos were located along the eastern and southern margins of the Colorado Plateau. The original Anasazi homeland had long been abandoned and was now thinly occupied by scattered bands of foraging people, ancestors of modern Navajo and Apache tribes and perhaps of Paiutes and Utes as well. Some Pueblo towns that he visited, still occupied today, were already hundreds of years old. During the next half

15. Zuni Pueblo. Photo by Ben Wittick, ca. 1890. School of American Research Collections at the Museum of New Mexico, Santa Fe. A small dance plaza is surrounded by houses whose rooftops and upper terraces are used as work areas, to sun dry fruit, and as viewing places for visitors to the sacred dance ceremonies.

century, other Spanish explorers recorded sometimes conflicting data about the Pueblos. Their estimates of population ranged from 20,000 to 250,000 people, living in perhaps 135 towns. Modern archaeology and analysis of historical records generally confirm the number of sixteenth-century communities and conservatively support a population estimate of 100,000 Anasazi people.

All pueblos described in the sixteenth century had similar economic, political, social, and ritual systems, but they spoke a number of different languages, suggesting a very complex history. No pueblo had a population much greater than about 3,000 but, in some instances, the Spanish reported that several towns were united into a single community of 10,000 or more people. In all other cases, political, economic, and social alliances among the pueblos were loose and cut across linguistic lines. Each was an essentially independent community of subsistence farmers with a theocratic government. Leadership was held by elders, and societies were economically and socially egalitarian, at least in principal.

All members of a community seemed to be active in ritual life, and religious rituals were generally directed toward maintaining a harmony with nature that was manifested by timely rainfall, agricultural success, and good health. Religion permeated all things. Villages might be cosmic maps; colors, numbers, and animals were sacred; beauty itself was a prayer, as were abstract images of clouds, lightning, and feathers. Deities called *kachinas* impersonated by masked dancers were of great importance at many Pueblos, as they are even to the present day. Kachinas are complex personages: they are ancestors, the unborn, and "Cloud People" who control weather and fertility. But, beyond the metaphysical, kachinas have overwhelming social impact; they touch upon all aspects of community life in those places where all people are required to participate in the Kachina Societies.

Social organizations varied, but rules of inheritance were universally important, regulating social position, marriage, membership in religious societies, and use of agricultural land. Gender was also an important regulatory factor. The woven and painted textiles made by the men and the pottery made by the women were traded

16. Field drawing of a mural showing a textile painted with a design similar to that used in Sikyatki-style Hopi pottery. Kiva 8, level 20 (or Kiva 9, level 1 which underlay Kiva 8), Pottery Mound, Rio Grande district, New Mexico, Pueblo IV, fifteenth century. Original painting about 4' high.

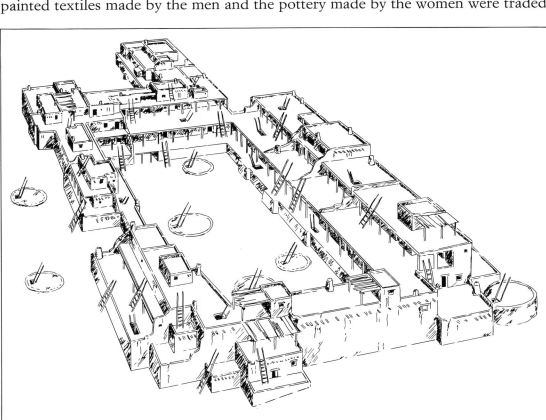

17. The main plaza of Pecos Pueblo at about the time of Spanish contact in 1540.

18. Pueblo IV ruin at San Juan Mesa, Jemez Mountains, New Mexico.

for hundreds of miles in all directions. Together with surplus foods, cured skins, turquoise, and other raw materials and manufactured objects, these comprised the material bases for trade with local people as well as with those living in distant parts of North and Middle America. Ritual knowledge also had economic value.

Most towns were made up of a few multistoried, terraced buildings, some had hundreds of rooms, arranged about plazas containing large ritual structures called *kivas*, which were the focus of community life. Depending on available materials, the buildings were of drywall masonry or of adobe. Many were defensive in character, built atop high cliffs, with few openings to the outside, and with limited access to dwellings even from within the walls. They were defended by members of War Societies. The Pueblos were ambivalent about violence; the Spanish described them as peaceful, even as they praised their skill as warriors. Quantities of food and water sufficient to withstand a siege, and, perhaps more importantly, the effects of droughts that might last for several years, were routinely stored within towns.

Food production techniques varied from place to place; ditch irrigation was practised along the Rio Grande, dry farming on the Hopi Mesas, and each special technique called for its own hybrid seed stock. Maize, beans, and squash were the staples, and cotton, tobacco, sunflowers, and other crops were also cultivated. Many wild plants such as amaranth were gathered for food, medicine, and to be processed and made into artifacts. Dogs and turkeys were the only domestic animals, and exotic birds, such as eagles and Mexican macaws, were kept for ritual purposes. Hunting provided most of the animal protein.

Sheep, horses, cattle, wheat, and fruit trees, as well as metal tools were introduced by the sixteenth-century Spanish colonists, who imposed their own legal system upon the Pueblos. Franciscan missionaries came also to convert the Indians to Catholicism, and they built large mission churches at a number of Pueblos during the first half of the seventeenth century. New diseases were introduced as well, and smallpox began to decimate Pueblo towns during that same period. Meanwhile, the easternmost of the Pueblos suffered from raids carried out by Apache bands and other tribes whose warfare practices had been revolutionized by their acquisition of horses.

These stresses primed the Pueblo Revolt of 1680, which drove the Spanish out of Pueblo territory, but religious friction with Christian missionaries was the trigger. When Franciscans burned kachina masks and forbade the sacred dances, they not only disrupted rituals designed to maintain universal harmony and preserve all life, but they also struck at the very core of Pueblo social unity. After the 1692 reconquest, only those missionaries who understood and were tolerant of the Pueblo lifeway could stay among them. But, from the time of the reconquest, the Anasazi era was truly finished for, ever since then, the Pueblo people have been a political minority in their own land.

19. Pottery bowls of the
Cibola/Chaco tradition. Left:
Chaco black-on-white, ht. 3",
ca. 1050-1250; right: Puerco
black-on-white, ht. 4 1/2", ca.
950-1100. Both northwestern
New Mexico. Laboratory of
Anthropology, Museum of
New Mexico, Santa Fe.

20. Two bracelets of "glycymeris" shell from the Gulf of California with bird and snake designs. Diameter about 4". Colonial period, Hohokam, ca. 800-900. Laboratory of Anthropology, Museum of New Mexico, Santa Fe.

21. *Two Hohokam red-on-buff pottery vessels. The bird effigy jar is about 8" high. Both are Colonial period, ca. 800-900. Laboratory of Anthropology, Museum of New Mexico, Santa Fe.*

22. *Pottery bowl, Mimbres black-on-white, Mimbres Branch of the Mogollon culture, southwestern New Mexico. Ht. 4 ¹/₄". Mimbres pottery art was strongly influenced by Anasazi aesthetics. Most painted bowls were ritually "killed" and buried with their dead. ca. 1100. Maxwell Museum of Anthropology, Albuquerque.*

23. 24. Top and side view of
a jar, Sikyatki polychrome
style with stylized birds,
feathers, dragonflies, and
textile patterns. From the
prehistoric Hopi town of
Sikyatki, northeastern
Arizona. Pueblo IV, fifteenth
to sixteenth century.
Diameter 15". University
Museum, University of
Pennsylvania.

Following pages:

25. Casas Grandes,
Chihuahua, northwestern
Mexico. In the foreground
are pens in which macaws
were kept to be traded to the
Anasazi and other
southwestern people. A
temple platform is in the
distance. ca. 1050-1360.

26. *Painting thought to be of a shaman with his animal familiar. Hog Springs, southern Utah, Archaic era. The "shaman" is about 7' high and painted with feathered strokes at the bottom so that it seems to merge with the rock.*

27. *Paintings at the "Great Gallery," Horseshoe Canyon, southern Utah, Archaic era, ca. 1000 B.C. Largest is about 10' high.*

Following pages:

28. *Rock engraving resembling a Mexican water deity. About 3' high. Jornado Mogollon, Three Rivers, southern New Mexico. ca. 1300.*

29. *Engraved stone, kachina mask. Ht. 28". From the Pueblo IV rock art site at Cerro de los Indios, middle Rio Grande district, New Mexico.*

30. The ruins of the Abo mission church at the Salinas Pueblo of Abo, New Mexico. ca. 1630-1670. The church was built according to plans of the Franciscan missionary in charge, but with native labor and building methods that were essentially Anasazi rather than European.

31. Aerial view of the Salinas Pueblo of Gran Quivira, New Mexico, abandoned ca. 1670. The excavated fifteenth to seventeenth centuries Indian community (Mound 7) is at the bottom. Foundations of an early seventeenth-century Spanish mission church is to the left and the later large mission church is in the upper part of the picture.

Chapter Two
THE ANASAZI WORLD: FROM EMERGENCE TO ABOUT A.D. 1000

Anasazi Origins and Pueblo Traditional Histories

Each of the Pueblos tells its own origin story, describing a journey upwards, usually through three Underworlds to this, the fourth level. Some myths tell of other levels above this one and predict more journeys to come. This earth is conceived of as the Mother, the sun, the Father, and the journeys upward through darkness are toward Mother Earth and Father Sun or, sometimes, Father Sky.

The people in these legends are initially unformed, unfinished, raw. They evolve, become more human, more finished at each stage as they move upward toward the light. They suffer and are endangered, they may fight, do evil, be punished, and not all survive. And, always, they communicate with, interact with, and require assistance from deities, birds, insects, other animals, and culture heroes. As they become more human, people may lose their ability to discourse with animals and the supernaturals and may even lose their position in nature. Esoteric rituals and intermediaries must replace the once commonplace relationships, and these become ever more important in maintaining or recreating the harmony with all things that is essential for a good and successful life.

The Place of Emergence from the last Underworld differs from group to group, but it is known, sacred, the locus for religious pilgrimages, and may only be accessible to the initiated. It is usually a body of water—a lake on a mountain, or a river in a canyon—and it is almost always to the north, in the direction of the ancient Anasazi homeland. There may be as many Places of Emergence as there are Pueblos. In each case, it seems that when the people arrived at the surface of this world, they faced new dangers as they began a search for the Center Place or Earth Navel, aided again by supernaturals, heroes, and animals. When the Center Place was finally located, it became the permanent home site of the group. Thus, every pueblo may be a sacred place, an Earth Navel, bounded by four distant and sacred mountains which define the home territory of a people.

Little that happened before the Emergence can be located in historic time or space, and the basic Emergence Myth is so widely shared among native North Americans as to suggest an antiquity that makes historic time and space irrelevant. However, the locations of many places mentioned in the post-Emergence tales are known. Some are identified with Anasazi sites, others with the ruins of different ancient southwestern cultures. Many are now religious shrines marking memorable places or events that occurred during a people's search for the Center. Such locations may be within or outside the boundaries of the sacred mountains. Many of these sites, which have been dated by modern archaeological methods, are certainly prehistoric and belong to the Anasazi periods that we call Pueblo III or Pueblo IV, dating from the years between the twelfth and the fifteenth centuries of our era. The search for the Center, if not the Emergence itself, appears to have begun during the time when Anasazi people were on the move away from the Colorado Plateau and toward their present homes.

Among Pueblos that are organized into clans, each clan has its own origin legend. All Pueblos have esoteric religious, ritual, and curing societies; each of these also has its own origin story; and the many rituals performed by such groups are likewise sanctioned by myth. In all of these cases, the myths involve the adventures of ordinary people and animals, culture heroes, and deities, and they often have the quality of historical legend. Real world locations where mythic events have taken place may be known to initiates and marked by shrines, and dates of the events may sometimes be surmised. It is possible, then, for there to be concordance amongst different legendary histories and Euro-American historicism.

Living people know history. Pueblo elders recount events that were told to them decades ago by, now-dead elders. The rhetoric may be somewhat different from that of more ancient tales, but many of these oral histories are verified and brought within the scope of Euro-American history by their intersection with written documents. The last mythic trek on foot to gather shells on the shores of the Pacific Ocean seems to have taken place for one group at the time of the 1849 Gold Rush. The last legendary bison hunt to the Plains appears to have occurred during the American Civil War. The Hopi-Tewa migration from the Rio Grande to their present villages in Arizona took place early in the eighteenth century. The Hopi town of Awatovi was destroyed by other Hopis for its ritual transgressions in about 1700. The Pecos people took refuge at Jemez Pueblo shortly after 1838 when their town was abandoned.

Sometimes, though, even modern history may be lost. No one can now be certain why the Laguna Pueblo colony that moved to Isleta Pueblo in the nineteenth century named their suburb after the ancient Hopi town of Oraibi, and there are conflicting stories about why a twentieth-century Laguna village is named after the American city of Philadelphia.

Traditional Pueblo histories may improve our understanding of Anasazi history and help in its reconstruction. The Zuni Place of Emergence is a known location far to the northwest of Zuni in the Grand Canyon. The Zuni Emergence seems to have taken place in about the twelfth century of our era; the search for the Center Place took generations, and the route is known and marked by shrines, some of which are datable Anasazi sites. But even though all Zuni people may acknowledge one Place of Emergence and one journey in search of the Center Place, some Zuni clans and ritual societies have other, contradictory origin stories. These may tell of roughly contemporaneous wanderings by people from the south of Zuni, and they are convincingly documented by shrines and archaeological sites that may be identified with Mogollon or Salado culture rather than that of the Anasazi.[1]

The simplest explanation for the contradictions is also the most useful: accept all versions as true. Assume that the original Zuni emerged from the Grand Canyon, searched for and found the Center Place, settled there, and afterwards were joined by other people from other places who were integrated into Zuni society without loss of self-identity.

As Zuni people, they accept the truth of the Zuni origin legend; as members of separate clans or esoteric societies they retain special histories which are also true. There is no need to replace one truth with another, for the Pueblo of Zuni is the sum of these diversities. All evidence—linguistic, archaeological, sociological, traditional—supports such an explanation. It becomes clear that Zuni has a long history of accommodating ethnic and ritual diversity, and similar accommodations appear to be the rule at most other Pueblos. If what appears to be true of Zuni and the other Pueblos was generally true throughout the Anasazi past, then we have a means to interpret Anasazi history as it is preserved in the archaeological record. It is a story of the fusion of diverse peoples into a unified whole, each group retaining its special character while joining the others in search of harmony with all things in the universe.

The Archaic Period

In 1927, a group of scholars met informally at the ruins of Pecos Pueblo[2] to discuss ongoing prehistoric research in the Southwest and agreed upon a framework, now called "the Pecos Classification," (see figure 9 on page 36) of the ancient culture history of the region. The Pecos outline named the earliest Anasazi stage "Basket Maker II," postulating a preagricultural "Basket Maker I" period. Basket Maker I proved elusive until the realization that it was identical to a late Archaic stage originally described hardly more than a decade after the first Pecos Conference.

Recognition that the Archaic was directly ancestral to any later southwestern people was made difficult because transition to a sedentary life based upon agricultural food production was gradual, and left few distinctive tangible remains. The earliest southwestern agriculturalists were the Archaic people who cultivated primitive varieties of maize before 1000 B.C. with little more care than they gave to nurturing the wild plants that were vital to their diet. Conversely, Basket Maker II farmers depended at least as much on wild plants for their sustenance as they did on cultivated crops. Their houses and food storage buildings were scarcely more elaborate than those of late Cochise and Oshara peoples, and their diets, food processing methods, and tools were also very similar.

Evidence that maize and squash were grown as supplemental foods in the Southwest and northern Mexico as early as 1000 B.C. comes from highland cave sites in both the Cochise and the Oshara regions. Along with beans, these domesticated plants had made possible the burgeoning civilizations of Mesoamerica and central Mexico. But, in the absence of great economic stress, there was little reason for any Archaic people of the sparsely populated deserts to commit themselves to the rigor and rhythms of a sedentary life dependent upon food production. So long as wild resources and population were in balance, southwestern Archaic life had many advantages over a more sedentary existence.

Because the ecology of their land varied so greatly, a wide range of animal and vegetable resources and climatic conditions were available to the Archaic people. Distance between resource areas was relatively short, and they could move easily from place to place within well-defined territorial ranges as different foods ripened and the seasons changed. Assuming low population density, foraging and hunting allowed for a comfortable, healthy, and secure life, with considerably less work than is generally the case for intensive agricultural production in that land.

The success of the Archaic life-style may be measured by the increase in population throughout western North America that occurred during that era. That success inevitably led to change, and the investments made by Cochise and Oshara people in food production and food storage increased in response to a growing imbalance of population size and wild food resources. The small, circular shelters of brush and mud built by Cochise people as early as 2500 B.C. were replaced by more substantial food storage structures and larger and more permanent dwellings at about the time when they first began to grow maize.

The number of their sites increased, as did the elaboration and quantity of their tools, which now included a variety of food-grinding stones, each type characteristic of a different time period or region. Their chipped stone knives, hide scrapers, dart points, spear points, and other hunting implements were far more variable in form, if less delicately made, than in the Paleo-Indian past. Meanwhile, along with rock art, a wealth of generally fragmentary baskets, cordage, finger-woven textiles, sandals, mats, and wood figurines preserved in dry caves provides us with a much broader picture of Archaic life than is currently available for any earlier native American people.

By about 500 B.C. some Cochise people were virtually sedentary and dependent upon horticulture. Shortly afterwards, they added pottery to their technological skills and, from then on, their archaeological remains are so different as to require cultural reclassification. These late Cochise groups are identical to the earliest Mogollon peoples and some Hohokam ones. The Oshara Archaic lagged somewhat in a similar drift toward sedentism, which was certainly influenced by, and perhaps channelled through, the Cochise-Mogollon. They were growing corn and squash before 500 B.C. and, by A.D. 200 or even earlier, their farming villages on the Colorado Plateau could be identified with the earliest Anasazi of the Basket Maker II period.

Glimpses of the intellectual and ceremonial life of these late Archaic people are visible to us through their art. Virtually all of their known pictorial art is in the form of pictographs and petroglyphs—rock art media that are notoriously difficult to date or even to attribute to any given culture.

Rock art thought to be Archaic is usually found in clusters rather than as isolated images. Much of it is in open sites, and many of these are near springs, ponds, or game trails, suggesting hunting associations. It is found in canyons and caves as well. Some rock shelters in isolated canyons on the Colorado Plateau and in caves in the Grand Canyon contain magnificent groups of paintings that are thought to date from about the first millenium B.C., logically identifying them with the Oshara tradition.

This art includes both realistic, action-packed pictures of humans and animals, and large, abstracted anthropomorphs. Some spectral figures appear to be in trancelike, shamanic states, and may be accompanied by animals similar to those that guide the shamans of modern hunting-gathering societies on their "Spirit Voyages." Similar paintings, which are related to Archaic traditions of northern Mexico, are found in caves along the Rio Grande in southwest Texas, and these may even relate to widespread ancient Mesoamerican hunting cults.

The wide distribution of this art lends support to the notion that the Archaic people of the Southwest were part of a large-scale, ideological network. Interpreting at least some of that art in terms of ritual interactions with Mesoamerica fits nicely with other evidence of early relationships between those regions. Most significantly, although these art forms and religious activities parallel the introduction of maize and the technology for growing it from Mexico, they do not seem to incorporate Mexican maize-related ritualism. Had agriculture been of greater importance to the Southwestern Archaic people, art and ritual associated with maize would probably have been more evident.

From earliest Basket Maker II times, beginning perhaps 2,000 years ago, the pace of change in the Anasazi way of life gradually accelerated as the Anasazi population increased and their territory expanded. Change was not uniform, and the qualities of economic, social, and ritual life, architecture, art, and technology that characterize each succeeding Anasazi period were not evenly distributed. As time passed, regional variations became increasingly marked, especially in styles of architecture and pottery design, as though self-identification were taking on new importance. The spread of Anasazi territory increased dramatically after about A.D. 900, as did the number and size of Anasazi communities and their population densities. To some degree, these increases were surely a consequence of emulation, as people living on the fringes of the Anasazi world adapted Anasazi solutions to the problems of daily life.

At first, the Anasazi were undistinctive. The near identity of Basket Maker II to the late Archaic is dramatized by the wide range of dates assigned by different and equally respected scholars to the beginning of the era—from 700 B.C. to A.D. 200.[3] In contrast, all agree[4] that the transition from Basket Maker II to Basket Maker III took place between A.D. 400 and 500. Evidence of Basket Maker II occupations comes from relatively few cave sites and rock shelters along the drainage of the San Juan River and from open sites in the Rio Grande Valley as far south as modern Albuquerque. These early villages may have been occupied only seasonally by people who planted maize and squash but still relied on hunting and foraging for their sustenance.

A village might include a few low, roughly circular houses called "pit houses" that were excavated into the ground. These were often about seven feet across; some were lined with stone slabs; and most had wood and adobe or wattle and daub (called "jacal") upper walls and roofs. Each had a fire pit, and entry was usually by way of a ladder placed through a smoke hole in the roof, or through a tunnellike, east-facing side entry. Some large pit houses are thought to have been ceremonial rooms. The only other Basket Maker II structures were small, slab-lined food storage cists that are almost indistinguishable from residences. The architecture shows no evidence of social differentiation, little in the way of ritual specialization and, except for villages in rock shelters that are patterned by the configuration of their building sites, no clearly discernable village plan.

Pottery was not made until the transition to Basket Maker III, but the decorated baskets which give the era its name are quite fine, as are sandals and other woven products. Cordage and netting are among other perishable materials preserved within the dry Basket Maker II rock shelters. Stone tools are not greatly different from those of the late Archaic. Even the earliest Anasazi baskets and textiles show stylistic maturity and a rigidly structured decorative system in which a limited number of geometric motifs are repeated within evenly spaced and well defined decorative zones. The arithmetically logical rhythms, inversions, and symmetries of this system, as well as its motifs and design elements, provided the basis for later Anasazi pottery-painting traditions.

Some rock art found on cliff surfaces near Basket Maker II villages is similar to late Archaic art. Pictures of broad-shouldered humans with trapezoidal torsos and gigantic hands and feet are distinctive. They sometimes wear elaborate headdresses, hair ornaments, earrings, necklaces, and sashes. Though some are large, most are considerably smaller and more detailed than in late Archaic paintings, and they tend to interact with each other more often and more obviously. These factors, combined with proximity to the villages, reduce their mystical qualities; they are less ethereal,

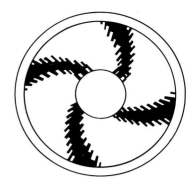

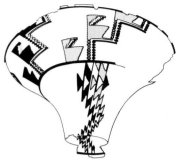

19. Basket Maker II and III basketry designs. The structural principles and geometric regularity of all later Anasazi and Pueblo decorative patterning were well established from the very beginning of the Anasazi era. Top: Peabody Museum, Harvard University. Bottom: University of Colorado Museum, diam. 31 ½".

20. Late Archaic or Basket Maker II engraved rock art. Original at Butler Wash near the San Juan River in southeastern Utah. Tallest figure, about 7'.

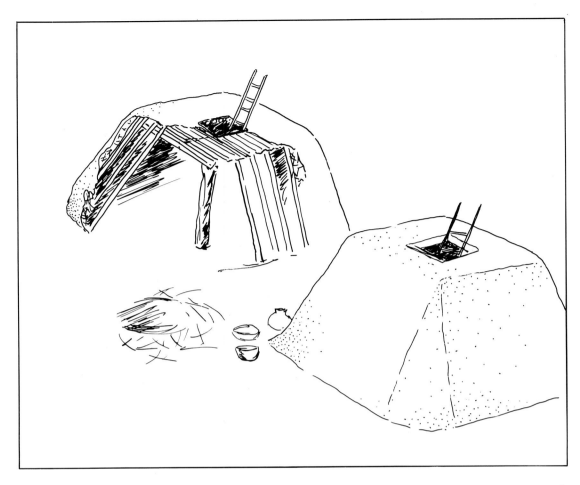

less forbidding, and more human than their Archaic counterparts, more a part of, than apart from the ordinary life of the community.

A more sedentary life, distinctive in many respects from the earlier period, characterizes Basket Maker III (A.D. 400/500-700/750). There were many more villages, larger and more widely distributed than during Basket Maker II, and virtually all had within them ritual rooms that we call *kivas* after their modern Pueblo equivalents. Pit houses were more complex, spacious and often deeper than in the past. Their earth-covered wooden roofs were supported by four posts and cross beams, or were dome-shaped, made by cribbing logs that rested upon pilasters. Many had storage bins, benches, a central fire pit, and a draft deflector between the fire and a ventilator shaft in one wall. As in earlier times, entry was by ladder from a centrally located roof hatch, or through an east-facing side entrance.

There were many outdoor work and cooking areas within a village. Surface buildings included slab-lined, jacal storage units, and roofed, open-walled structures called *ramadas* that shaded work areas and living spaces. Some kivas were modified residences with similar architectural features, but many were larger than houses, some as big as thirty-five feet across. Many houses and most kivas had small, carefully excavated holes located near the center of the floor, in which turquoise or other offerings were placed. This seems to have served as a *sipapu*, symbolic today of the opening to the last Underworld from whence people emerged. On death, people were buried within or very near to a village, often on the floor of an abandoned house or in a storage cist. They were usually layed out with knees bent, in a prenatal position. Infant mortality was high, and relatively few people lived to be very old. Burial offerings included tools and baskets or pottery bowls, which may have held food. Most of the people were relatively short and stocky, very much like their modern-day Pueblo descendants.

22. Basket Maker III basket from Broken Flute Cave, Four Corners region. Ht. 12″. American Museum of Natural History, New York.

23. Pottery bowl, Cibola/ Chaco tradition, La Plata black-on-white. Ht. 3″. Basket Maker III, ca. 600-800. Laboratory of Anthropology, Museum of New Mexico, Santa Fe.

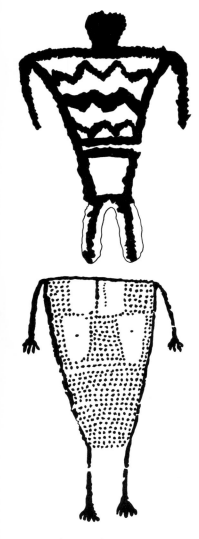

Agricultural fields were located near villages and, in some areas, check dams and other water control devices were built and maintained to help secure agricultural success. Farming was now of fundamental importance, but hunting and gathering continued to provide vital dietary supplements. Protein-rich beans were added to the inventory of cultivated foods in about A.D. 600, and cotton and the bow-and-arrow came into general use in the next century, during the transition to the Pueblo I period. These changes were echoed by changes in the appearance of stone tools: small, notched arrow points became commonplace, and two-handed grinding stones (called *manos*) were used to grind maize on large, wide stone mortars (called *metates*). These replaced the one-handed manos and bowllike mortars that had been used for millennia to process wild vegetable foods. Virtually all of these novelties ultimately derived from Mexico, but the mechanisms for their introduction to the Anasazi are unknown. Trade was widespread; turquoise and ocean shells are among exotic materials from different parts of the Southwest, far west, and Mexico that are found at many sites.

Basketry, sandal making, weaving, and most other industries of earlier times continued with great elaboration. Turkey feathers and strips of rabbit fur were woven into warm robes, and other woven clothing included beautifully decorated shirts and aprons. Pottery for water and food storage, cooking, food service, ritual, and trade became a major home industry. The earliest ceramics are Mogollon-like, red- and brown-wares, but varieties of hand-built white or gray pottery decorated with black, painted lines became increasingly popular during this period. As time passed, black-on-white pottery became a hallmark of the Anasazi on the Colorado Plateau.

There were many more perishable and ephemeral objects made than we know of. Body paint, shield paintings, decorated clothing, and elaborate feather ornaments are shown in rock art, but few actual examples survive. Animal skins and many kinds of wooden objects were carved, painted, and constructed for social and ritual

24. Basket Maker III costumes as shown in pictographs of painted or woven textiles. Both from Grand Gulch, southeastern Utah, approximately life-sized.

25. Fluteplayer figures, animals, and other petroglyphs, probably Pueblo II. Original at Sand Island, on the San Juan River, Utah. ca. 6" high.

use, and ritual art may well have included pictures made of colored sands and other dry materials. Despite these elaborations, there still were few indications of social differences in architecture and other physical remains and, especially where villages were located in open sites, little obvious evidence of community planning.

There was further reduction in the size and mystical qualities of rock art and great increase in its quantity and variety. It was made near or within villages, or on boulders atop mesas, or near game trails or other open locations. Many new subjects were introduced, including birds and other animals, realistic hunting scenes, and flute-playing figures, variations of which persist to the present day. Human handprints, found in earlier rock art, were now made in great profusion, and were often repeated in clustered masses on cliff walls. The sum of these changes was to make Anasazi rock art increasingly more human, approachable, communal, and better integrated with everyday Anasazi life. These qualities conform to other Basket Maker III attributes: community life came to focus on home, kiva, and village. Kivas evolved from residences and their rituals apparently were kin-based and integrative. They seem to have directed the cooperative kin group toward actions designed to encourage and perhaps ensure agricultural success. In the arid Southwest that ultimately meant control over the elements, especially rainfall, and the sanctioning of social procedures to help people deal with crop failure and drought.

The Developmental Pueblo Period:[5] A.D. 700-1100

The foundations for Anasazi culture were laid during late Archaic and Basket Maker II times. It took on distinctive form during the Basket Maker III period and became firmly established in the succeeding era, between about A.D. 700 and 1100. Those 400 years are sometimes called the "Developmental Pueblo" period, incorporating within it both Pueblo I and Pueblo II of the Pecos Classification. In this time, there

26. Coombs Village, a Developmental Pueblo site in southern Utah, as it might have been in the early twelfth century.

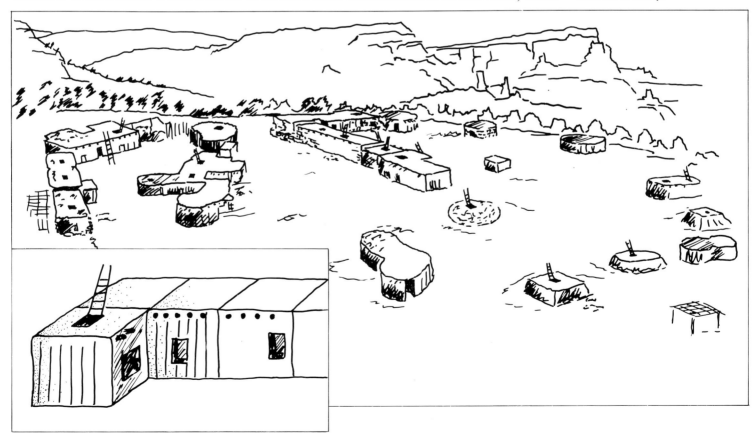

was a marked increase in the number of Anasazi communities. Alliance networks were established among some of them, local diversity and regionalism became marked, and there was considerable development of the two most visible Anasazi hallmarks: architecture and painted pottery.

Important architectural innovations began in Pueblo I with elaboration of the jacal and stone storage structures and brush and pole ramadas that had been surface features of Basket Maker III villages. As time passed, such surface buildings became more massive, were joined together, and, as multiroom structures called "unit houses" that grew by accretion, became virtually conterminous with each community. Ultimately, dry masonry or stone and adobe buildings, which incorporated many rooms within them, replaced pit houses as residences both in rock shelters and, most especially, at open sites on mesa tops or in valleys.

Where room allowed, buildings usually faced onto a courtyard or plaza located to the south or southeast, which held one or more kivas. Kiva architecture was elaborate, stylized, and variable. Most kivas were built with care and precision; some were large, but many were relatively small, built to accommodate a dozen or so individuals. Plaza areas were probably used as public ritual spaces, and house roofs replaced the open spaces of earlier pit house villages as outdoor living and work areas. After about A.D. 850 or 900, most Anasazi towns were highly structured communities built around plazas and kivas that were, both physically and spiritually, their centers.

Surface architecture developed gradually, and villages of the early Pueblo I period were not greatly different from those of Basket Maker III. As the Anasazi expanded, both through a natural increase of their population and by absorbing new peoples, a greater variety of geographical and ecological zones came to be included in their territory. This variety contributed to diversity, including diversity in the character of communities and their architecture. In new regions, adaptation of Anasazi ways—even after A.D. 1000—often had a Basket Maker quality, with transition to more contemporary modes perhaps compressed into only one or two generations.

Among the new Anasazi territories were mountain regions, such as those adjacent to the Rio Grande valley in northern New Mexico and in the southern and eastern parts of the Colorado Plateau. Some of these regions, such as the northern Rio Grande, retained a rustic quality for generations. These highlands often had short growing seasons, were forested, and had rich hunting and food gathering resource areas. Mountain slopes at elevations above 6,000 feet could usually depend on the summer rainfalls that were necessary for agricultural success, allowing for dry

27. Section of a pit house with a side entrance through an anteroom and vestibule.

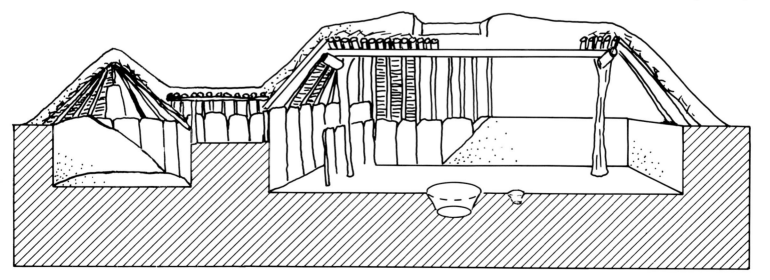

farming on relatively small clearings and mountain meadows. Water management was generally limited to placing lines of boulders at strategic locations as check dams to slow down water drainage following a rainstorm.

The high country could be very cold, making it necessary to dig pit houses deep for warmth, and to have within them large food storage bins for convenience when heavy snows limited access to the outdoors. Entry was often made through a tunnel and antechamber built to the east or southeast and, in heavily wooded areas, large beams were used to support massive, earth-covered wooden roofs. The similarities to some styles of Basket Maker III pit houses could be very close. Not all high country pit house villages were occupied during the winter months and, since frost came early and stayed long, growing seasons were short and there was great risk of losing crops to untimely weather. High risk of agricultural failure, fields that were limited in size and widely scattered, continued dependence on hunting and gathering, and seasonal migrations, all combined to keep population levels low and villages small. When population density increased, it became usual for larger villages to be built at lower elevations where the growing season was longer. New agricultural fields were then developed on alluvial plains.

Villages at lower elevations and in the arid mesa and canyon country of the Four Corners might have longer growing seasons, but rainfall was less certain, wild foods more scarce, and agricultural success depended on labor intensive water management and gardening techniques. Local droughts or untimely rainfall might cause crop failure for several consecutive years, making it necessary to store large quantities of food for long periods. Favored agricultural areas included mesa tops and alluvial fans that formed in stream beds, and where water poured off mesa tops following storms. Check dams, terraced fields, reservoirs, wells, and irrigation canals might all be built to manage scarce water. The need for large and secure storage spaces, for mutual aid during lengthy periods of drought, and for cooperative labor forces encouraged development of ever larger communities and of alliances among neighboring groups. Even so, a pattern began to emerge of periodic abandonment and reoccupation of canyons and mesa tops, especially in the Anasazi heartland where many villages of this era were lived in for only about thirty years.

Regional networks were organized in the Mesa Verde, Chaco Canyon, and Kayenta districts. In these areas, a relatively large number of kivas of various sizes and types are sometimes found in a single community, suggesting an elaboration of ritual institutions; and there was increasing specialization in production of pottery, ornaments, and woven goods. Cradle boards were now used for infants so that they could spend virtually all of their time with their mothers. A child's head bound to a

28. A child tied to a cradle board.

29. Cradle board, wooden rods tied to a wooden frame ca. 29″ long. (Replica.) The child would be tied to the cradle and the cradle carried by a tump-line visible at the bottom. The skull which shows cranial flattening induced by such a cradle is of an adult woman. Pueblo II.

30. Remains of jacal wall in a rock shelter, Grand Gulch, southeastern Utah, Mesa Verde-Kayenta borderlands. Wood and adobe, ca. 5' high. Pueblo III, ca. thirteenth-century. Note the Basket Maker III handprints partially covered by the later wall.

hard cradle board would be deformed, presumably with deliberation and for reasons of beauty. Ceremonialism was elaborated, and there was greater variety and formality in burial practices. All these factors combine to suggest increased social, political, and economic complexity and a deepening concern for family stability and religious ritual. Close parallels to historic era Pueblo ritualism and political and social organization become obvious for the first time.

The location of village sites, whether on mesa tops, mountain meadows, or valleys, and the special qualities of available building materials, had considerable effect on the evolving regional building styles. In the Kayenta and Mesa Verde areas, jacal and large sandstone blocks cemented with mud adobe were favored building materials. Thin slabs of laminar sandstone that were available in the southeastern San Juan Basin had a fundamental effect on Chacoan architectural styles, while adobe, cobblestones, and jacal characterize buildings of the Rio Grande district. Where there was regional scarcity of large trees for roof beams, rooms tended to be small or narrow, and engineering devices such as pilasters, cribbing, corbeling, and domes were used for roof support systems. Elsewhere, large beams resting on wooden posts that supported flat or cribbed roofs might allow for bigger rooms.

During this time, pottery painting became an important art medium that was both distinctively Anasazi and expressive of regional variation. Even taking regional variations into account, ceramic technologies were basically similar and highly conservative, with relatively few fundamental changes until the twentieth century. In most places, pottery was probably made and decorated by women who learned the craft from relatives. Vessels were constructed by hand, using coil methods, and then were fired in bonfire kilns, usually after all decoration had been applied. If vessels were to have painted designs, they were generally smoothed by scraping and then slipped, perhaps polished, and finally painted with a brush made of chewed yucca leaf.

Through time, an increasing proportion of pottery was painted, but most vessels were decorated by texturing rather than painting. Most painted wares were in the form of bowls and jars, decorated on one surface with linear designs. As the painting tradition matured, surfaces to be painted were treated with considerable care and slipped with a fine white or, much less often, red clay. From very early times, either

31. Domed roof made by corbeling wooden beams on stone pilasters. Upper kiva, Square Tower House, Mesa Verde. Photo by Jesse L. Nusbaum, 1907. Museum of New Mexico, Santa Fe. Nusbaum was an archaelogist who helped pioneer the restoration and stabilization of Anasazi ruins.

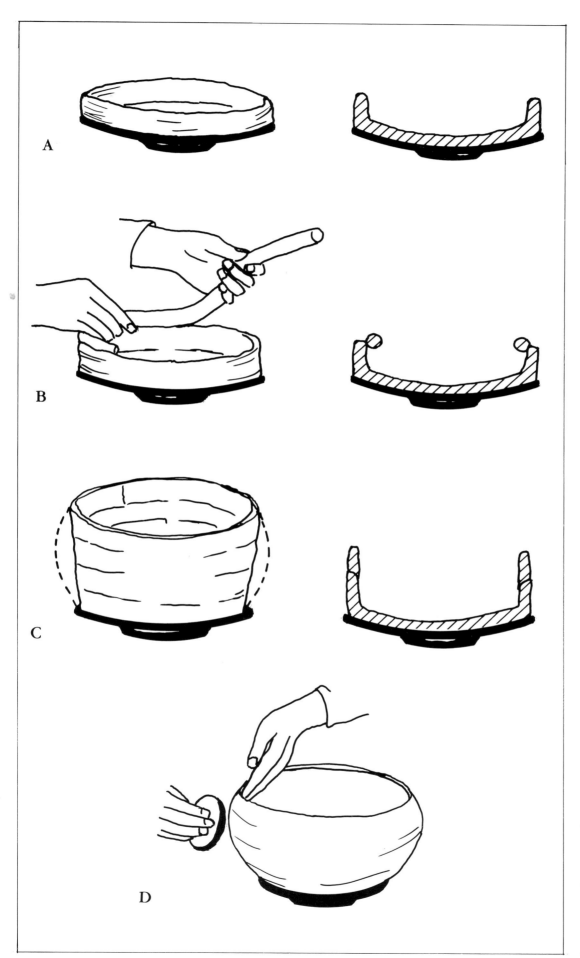

A

B

C

D

32. Pueblo pottery making continues Anasazi pottery-making methods with minor variations. The artist builds the vessel by adding coils of clay which are pressed together and then smoothed with shaped pieces of gourd. Final shaping involves pushing and scraping the clay with finger pressure and gourd tools.

33. Two pottery jars. Neck banded vessels such as these were among the most common Anasazi utility vessels from Basket Maker III through Pueblo I periods. Both from the Four Corners region. Ht. 6 ½″. Maxwell Museum of Anthropology, Albuquerque.

of two kinds of black paint, one organic and the other of iron-bearing minerals, were used in different regions.

A kind of formalism parallel to that of late Developmental Pueblo architecture is visible in the painted pottery of the period. Most pottery paintings relied on a limited number of geometric motifs placed within a few well-defined, framed panels or design zones. These were generally structured with arithmetic and symmetrical regularity and were often laid out and patterned to conform with and to reinforce vessel shape. The formal system and the iconography quite clearly derive from Basket Maker III textiles and baskets. Similar designs are still used by modern Pueblo people, who may identify them as abstract references to rain, lightning, clouds, and prayer feathers. Rarely, life forms were used decoratively within a design zone and, even more rarely, a painting of a human or other animal dominated a design area. Such images might resemble rock art but, as a rule, painted pottery of this era was elegantly rational and integrated with the picture surface.

In contrast, the visual relationships between a picture and the surface on which it was placed are forever uncertain in most Anasazi rock art where no clear boundaries inform the eye or mind where picture space begins or ends. Uncertainty about dating often makes it impossible to distinguish Basket Maker III from Developmental Pueblo rock art, but the shifts in form, content, and location that began in Basket Maker times seem to have simply continued. Whatever the ritual purposes rock art now served, they were compatible with the village orientation of Anasazi life and the change in the major locus of ritual expression from the outdoors to the kivas.

34. Pueblo I and II rock art, petroglyphs near the eleventh century Chaco outlier called Village of the Great Kivas, an ancestral site of modern Zuni Pueblo.

Regional Traditions and Neighboring Peoples

By the middle of the Developmental Pueblo period, kiva architecture had become one visible expression of regionalism. In the Kayenta district, kivas were small, either circular or rectangular, and their roofs were supported by four corner posts or

32. *Paintings at White Shaman Cave, junction of the Pecos and Rio Grande rivers, east of the Big Bend in southern Texas. Largest figure about 14' high. Archaic era, ca. 3000 B.C.*

33. *Paintings at the "Great Gallery," Horseshoe Canyon, southern Utah. Shaman figures about 10' high painted with feathered strokes so that they merge with the rock are at the right. Much smaller realistic men and animals are at the left. All seem to date from the Archaic era, ca. 1000 B.C.*

34. Pit house about 14' in diameter at Chaco Canyon, northwestern New Mexico. Note ventilator at top, stone air deflector, storage bins at each side of deflector, fire pit, ladderholes and "sipapu" along central axis. Post holes for the four-post roof support and storage pits are excavated into the floor. A grinding stone for corn meal is near the fire pit. Basket Maker III, eighth century.

Right and opposite, bottom:

35. Two gourd-shaped pottery ladles, Kayenta tradition, Kana-a black-on-white. ca. 7 ¹/₂" long. Basket Maker III, ca. 725-875. Laboratory of Anthropology, Museum of New Mexico, Santa Fe.

36. *Pottery Bowl, Cibola/
Chaco tradition, La Plata
black-on-white. The
asymmetrical design is
unusual and suggests an early
date. Ht. 3 ¹/₂". Basket
Maker III, ca. 600-800.
Laboratory of Anthropology,
Museum of New Mexico,
Santa Fe.*

Following pages:

37. *Wrapped weave sandals,
natural fibers. ca. 10" long.
Late Basket Maker II, San
Juan region. Laboratory of
Anthropology, Museum of
New Mexico, Santa Fe.*

38. *Carrying bag, finger
woven dyed fibers with
aboriginal repairs. A weasel
skin is sewn to it. Ht. 26".
Basket Maker II, southern
Utah. Laboratory of
Anthropology, Museum of
New Mexico, Santa Fe.*

39. *Habitation site at a rock
shelter, Natural Bridges,
southeastern Utah. The
roofless round structure is
unusual and the broad-
shouldered figures painted on
its walls are Basket Maker in
style. The patterned handprints along the back wall of
the shelter may also be
Basket Maker, but handprints
are typical of all Anasazi and
Pueblo eras.*

40. *Waterfall run-off from
the mesa-top following a
summer shower, Chaco
Canyon, New Mexico.*

41. *Check dams and
agricultural terraces, Gila
Mountains, New Mexico. ca.
eleventh century.*

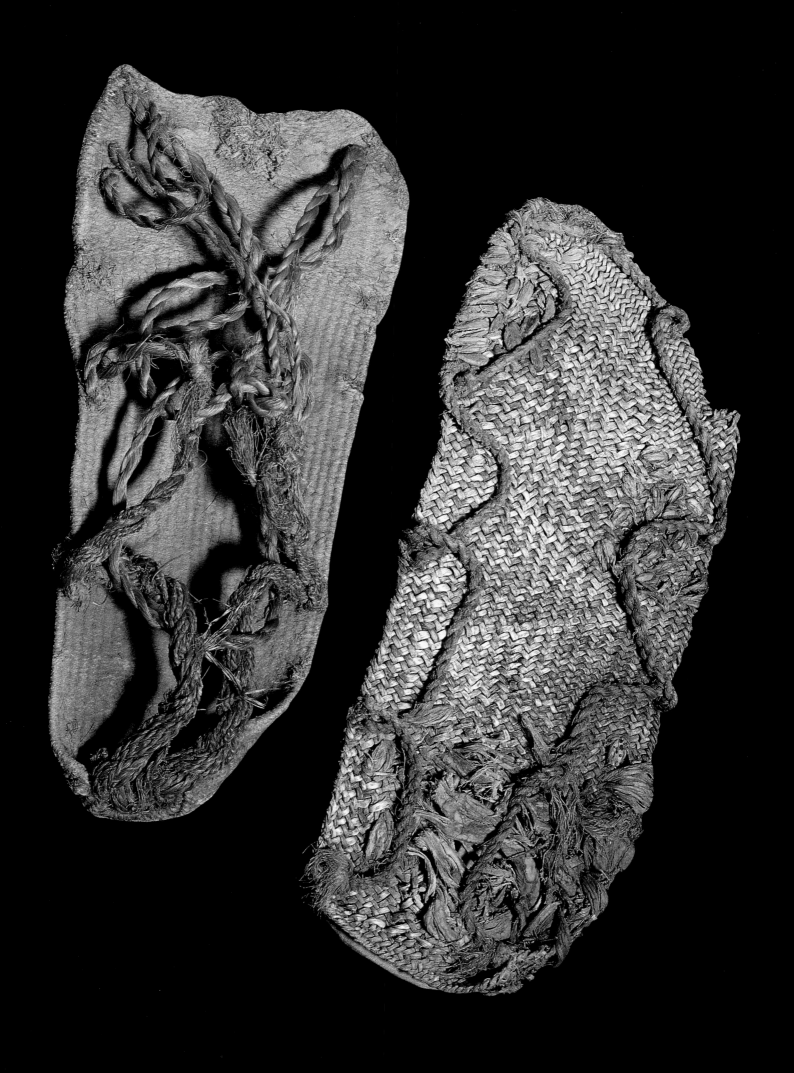

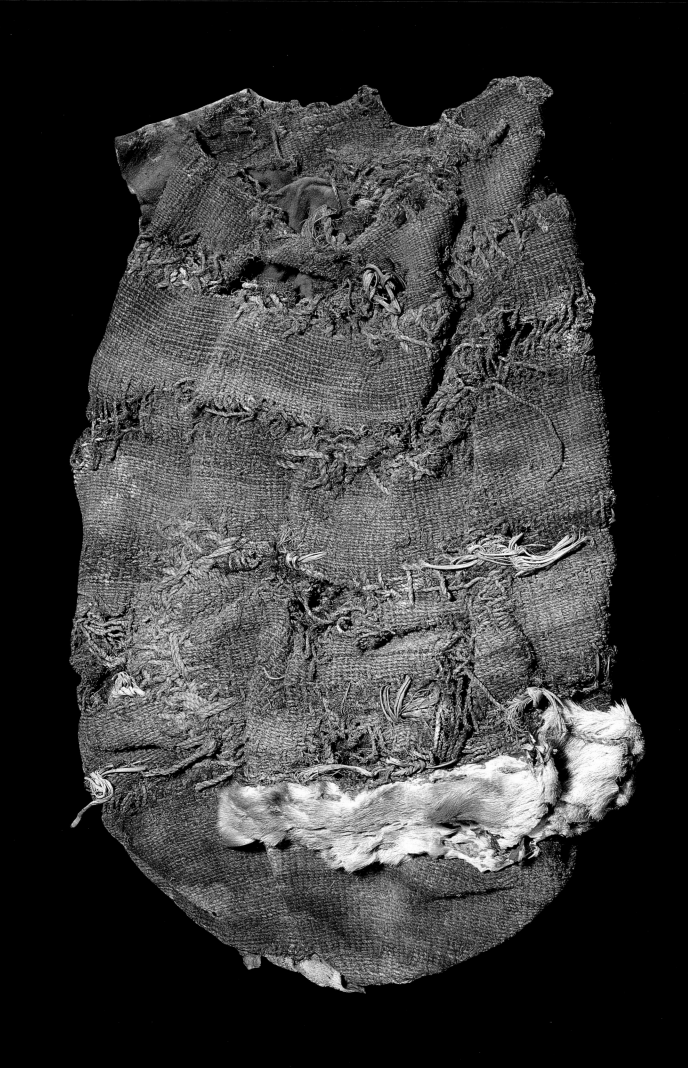

42. *Kiva, Twin Trees Site 102, Mesa Verde. Diameter ca. 14'. Kiva features include a narrow bench, and stone pilasters to support a cribbed wooden roof. A ventilator with a stone cover, fire pit and "sipapu" are along the central axis and a shallow trench that may be a foot drum is at the top. Pueblo I-II, ca. 900.*

43. *Deep pit house, Twin Trees Site 103. ca. 14' square. Remains of slab-lined storage bins are seen between the fire pit and the ventilator and many storage cysts are in the floor. In some places pit houses continued to be built until as late as the fifteenth century. Pueblo I, ca. 830.*

44. *Kiva, Ruins Road Site 16, Mesa Verde, Colorado. Diameter ca. 12'. Features are similar to those of the earlier Twin Trees Site 102 kiva (plate 42) but are more precisely defined. Pueblo II, eleventh century.*

45. *Coombs Village, Kayenta district, southern Utah (Reconstructed.) This is a typical Developmental Pueblo village. ca. 1050-1200.*

Following pages:

46. *Jacal wall of a room in a rock shelter at Grand Gulch, southeastern Utah, Mesa Verde-Kayenta borderlands. Wood and adobe, ca. 9' high.*

47. *Cibola/Chaco mineral-paint tradition, Red Mesa black-on-white jar. Ht. 11". ca. 870-950. Laboratory of Anthropology, Museum of New Mexico, Santa Fe.*

*48. Pueblo I and II pottery
vessels, Cibola/Chaco
mineral-paint tradition. From
left: Red Mesa black-on-
white bowl, ca. 870-950;
Cebolleta black-on-white
canteen, ca. 950-1100;
Kiatuthlana black-on-white
bowl, ca. 800-870. Canteen is
7" high. Laboratory of
Anthropology, Museum of
New Mexico, Santa Fe.*

*49. Double bowl, mineral-
painted pottery, Chaco/
Cibola tradition. White
Mound black-on-white.
Ht. 3 ¼". Basket Maker III
to Pueblo I, ca. 700.
Laboratory of Anthropology,
Museum of New Mexico,
Santa Fe.*

50. Basket Maker III to
Pueblo II pottery of the three
major Anasazi traditions.
Left to right: Cibola/Chaco
bowl, Red Mesa black-on-
white, ca. 870-950, from
Chaco Canyon; Mesa Verde
bowl, Mancos black-on-white,
ca. 950-1150; Kana-a black-
on-white seed jar, from the
Kayenta region, ca. 725-875.
The seed jar is 9" high.
Laboratory of Anthropology,
Museum of New Mexico,
Santa Fe.

51. Mesa Verde-style carbon-
paint pottery. McElmo black-
on-white bowl. 4 ½" deep.
Pueblo II, eleventh to twelfth
centuries. Laboratory of
Anthropology, Museum of
New Mexico, Santa Fe.

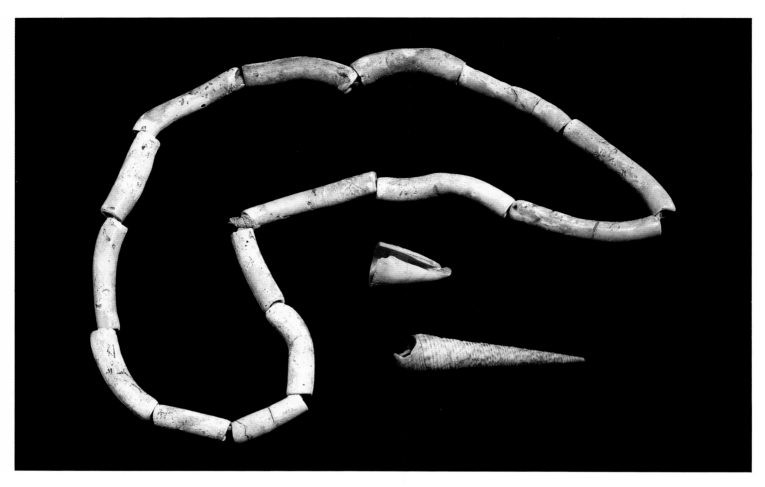

52. *Anasazi shell ornaments,*
necklace and two pendants.
Necklace 13" long. Pueblo II.
Laboratory of Anthropology,
Museum of New Mexico,
Santa Fe.

53. *Carved slate paint*
palette, turtle effigy stone
bowl (bottom), serrated stone
arrowhead, and clay figurine
fragment. Palette is 9 ¹/₂"
long. Hohokam, Colonial and
Sedentary periods. Maxwell
Museum of Anthropology,
Albuquerque.

by horizontal beams laid across pilasters. In the Mesa Verde district most kivas were small, round or keyhole shaped, and there were a great number of them, perhaps indicating many esoteric societies, clans, or other kin organizations. Their domed or cribbed roofs were often made of short logs laid across six evenly spaced stone pilasters, which sprang upward from benches jutting from their walls. In the south and east, in the Chaco Canyon, Cibola, and Rio Grande districts, kivas were round or rectangular; some were very large, and there was more variability in features such as benches and pilasters. Their roofs were generally flat and supported on beams that were carried by four evenly spaced posts set on the floor away from room walls.

Except in the Rio Grande, interior features such as deflectors, ventilators, benches, fire pits, altars, and foot drums were generally of stone and highly stylized. Kiva forms had clearly derived from residential pit houses, and many of their formal peculiarities were modelled upon earlier local solutions to practical problems of everyday life. New social and ritual meanings were now attached to various obsolete domestic architectural forms in different regions, and we can only make the assumption that these somehow responded to variant social and ritual practices of the different Anasazi peoples.

A northwest-southeast division developed in painted pottery traditions, but here, practical explanations for the origin of variation are wanting, while assumptions about social meanings are even more problematical. Initially, both areas used much the same fine-line, black-on-white designs and were distinguished primarily by their selection of organic or inorganic paint. However, by about A.D. 900, design differences became obvious in the two regions; they stemmed, to an increasing degree, from sensitive exploitation by artists of the unique qualities of their different paints, slips, and clays. Artistic variations in pottery painting were expressive of regional preferences in line quality, color, texture, and mass, rather than any more radical differences in style or iconography.

Kayenta and Mesa Verde potters placed great emphasis on heavy masses of carbon-based paint that fired with a soft, gray-to-black tone on white, polished surfaces. This promoted use of positive-negative designs in which figure-ground relationships are quite ambiguous. In the Chaco, Cibola, and Rio Grande areas, fine lines of iron-based, reddish-black paint were placed on surfaces that tended to be chalky white. Hachuring was often used, and the resulting designs depended on shades of gray and a rather tense linearity. The end products are quite different, even when identical motifs were used in similar configurations. As time passed, many variants of each style developed, each serving as a kind of signature to identify Anasazi subgroups. Some of these wares were widely traded, even outside Anasazi territories. Within the Anasazi world, that trade may have been for aesthetic or social purposes rather than for more practical reasons, since the utilitarian quality of the pottery was much the same in all regions.

Comparisons to other southwestern cultural traditions are informative. Hohokam architectural and agricultural modes, evolving as they did in the hot deserts of southern Arizona, had little impact upon the Anasazi. Their houses were designed for a much warmer climate than the Colorado Plateau, and their irrigation technology required broad, shallow rivers that flowed through wide expanses of flat land, features not found in the Anasazi country. Less easily explained is the absence of any influence of Hohokam ritual architecture and ritual practices upon the Anasazi. Nothing resembling Hohokam ball courts or truncated pyramids, both presumably derived from Mesoamerica, are found at any early Anasazi site. The Anasazi buried their dead, while the Hohokam practised cremation and urn burial; and Hohokam priestly paraphernalia, such as palettes, pyrite mirrors, stone bowls, and figurines, are generally unknown at Anasazi sites. However, luxury items,

35. Regional variations in Pueblo II and III kiva architectural styles, and a composite of a Chaco-style Great Kiva. The three small kivas are each about 14′ in diameter, the Great Kiva about 45′. (Small Kiva drawings after Ferguson and Rohn: 1987.)

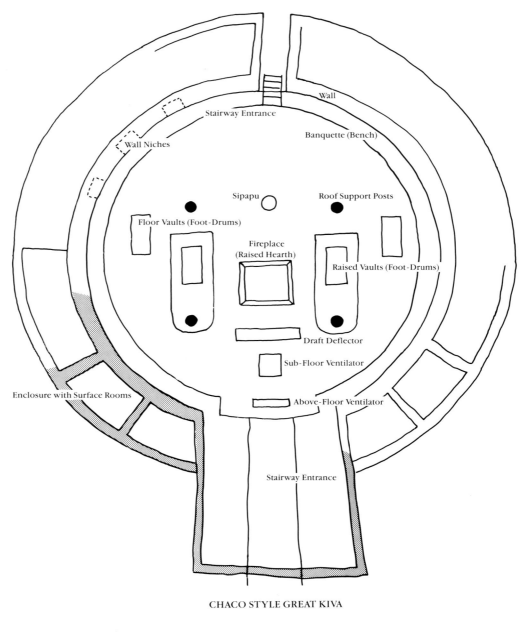

Wall

Stairway Entrance

Wall Niches

Banquette (Bench)

Sipapu

Roof Support Posts

Floor Vaults (Foot-Drums)

Fireplace (Raised Hearth)

Raised Vaults (Foot-Drums)

Draft Deflector

Sub-Floor Ventilator

Enclosure with Surface Rooms

Above-Floor Ventilator

N

Stairway Entrance

CHACO STYLE GREAT KIVA

Niche

Banquette   Sipapu

Pilaster

Hearth

Deflector

Recess

Ventilator

MESA VERDE STYLE KIVA

Hearth

Deflector

Roof Support Post

Recess

Ventilator

KAYENTA STYLE KIVA

Sipapu

Banquette

Hearth

Deflector

Recess

Pilaster

Ventilator

CHACO STYLE KIVA

36. Pueblo II pottery of the Kayenta mineral-paint tradition. Flagstaff black-on-white bowl, ca. 1100-1200; Walnut black-on-white mug, ca. 1100-1125. Mug is 7″ high. Laboratory of Anthropology, Museum of New Mexico, Santa Fe.

37. Rio Grande version of Red Mesa black-on-white canteen, northern New Mexico. Ht. 8 ¹/₂″. Pueblo II, tenth century. Maxwell Museum of Anthropology, Albuquerque.

including Anasazi turquoise and jet ornaments, and Hohokam shell jewelry and cotton, were exchanged, suggesting that highly selective historical processes were at work.

Those Hohokam who moved northward during their Colonial period, through the Verde Valley to the Mogollon Rim, found it necessary to change their agricultural and architectural habits. Their houses were more substantial, and water management techniques were considerably modified in the higher elevations. But, even though they adopted some methods from their Mogollon, Sinagua, and Anasazi neighbors and exchanged practical and luxury goods with them, their spiritual practices show little northern influence. There are no Hohokam kivas, and there are few ritual objects that resemble those of Anasazi, Sinagua, or Mogollon people. Again, a clear pattern of ethnic choice is visible.

Hohokam painted pottery may be the oldest in the Southwest and is the most distinctive technically, stylistically, and iconographically. It shows remarkable consistency in all periods, and is the only southwestern tradition to use the paddle-and-anvil finishing procedures of northwestern Mexico. It also resembles Mexican wares in its use of red or brown paint on red, brown, or buff clay bodies. Spontaneous brush handling, broad, red lines, preferences for overall patterning and expanding designs, as opposed to zonal subdivisions and restricted pictorial fields, are other characteristics distinguishing Hohokam from Anasazi painted pottery. Similarities to Anasazi traditions involve use of similar motifs and compositional systems that were, in fact, commonly used throughout the north Mexican frontier.

Interior surfaces of Hohokam painted bowls were often divided into four or more even-sized segments that radiated outward from the center to a weakly framed or, sometimes, an unframed rim. Exterior surfaces of jars were often covered by diagonally organized repeat patterns or ringed by concentric bands or registers. In

38. Small helmet-shaped Hohokam pottery bowl with dancing figures. Ht. 5".
Laboratory of Anthropology, Museum of New Mexico, Santa Fe.

either case, small-scale motifs that spiral outward or upward, or any other compositional system that had the potential to expand infinitely beyond the bounds of a vessel surface might be used.

Perhaps nothing better illustrates the distinctive qualities of Anasazi and Hohokam painting styles than the contrasting ways in which the two groups handled designs that were virtually identical. The Hohokam aesthetic goal seemed to be always to create open-ended harmonic compositions by repeating design units in potentially infinite sequences. Visual interest depended on use of a lively line and subtle variations in scale. The harmony of Anasazi designs depended instead on patterning limited numbers of design zones, each filled with several tightly drawn, small-scale design units. It was a visually complex but closed system. Hohokam pottery painting appears to be spontaneous and casual; Anasazi pottery painting is studied and controlled.

As with most other prehistoric painted pottery of the Southwest and northern Mexico, Hohokam wares were household workshop products, utilitarian containers decorated more or less skillfully according to the tenets of some local variation of a widespread tradition. As elsewhere, innovations show concern for making pictures that transcend the utilitarian character of the vessel and some subjects, including lively images of birds, humans, and lizards, are clearly related to some of their rock art. Other rock art pictures include circles, spirals, and squiggles, usually painted with broad, spontaneous brown lines that resemble the brushwork of their paintings on pottery. Rock art compositions tend to ramble over unframed surfaces.

In contrast to the Hohokam, many Mogollon farmers were not only direct neighbors of the Anasazi, but those living in high mountain country shared demanding environments with them. Without doubt, the earliest Anasazi were very heavily influenced by neighboring Mogollon people. The material remains of the southernmost Basket Maker II people are almost indistinguishable from those of the northernmost Mogollon, and many Basket Maker III and Developmental Pueblo villages closely resemble both earlier and contemporaneous mountain Mogollon communities. Anasazi pottery making and agriculture were apparently learned from the Mogollon; their rectangular kivas resemble earlier Mogollon ceremonial rooms, and other ritual similarities include mortuary offerings and mortuary practices.

There were important differences also. Mogollon communities usually persisted as pit house villages long after the Anasazi were building multiroom pueblos, and Anasazi ritual architecture became far more elaborate than that of the Mogollon. While Mogollon pottery was technically similar to Anasazi wares in most respects, it was usually brown or red, quite similar from place to place, and generally less diversified in its decoration. Pottery painting was not widely practised by any Mogollon group before about A.D. 950, and earlier painted wares generally resemble Hohokam or north Mexican types. Most Mogollon rock art made prior to A.D. 1000 was also unlike Anasazi art. In the mountainous west-central regions, Mogollon artists painted simple human and animal stick figures in red on the rock walls of isolated canyons. In the eastern desert parts of their territory, where agriculture was probably less important then hunting and gathering, their rock art seems to be an extension of late Archaic pictorial traditions.

Anasazi rock art of this era, which differs from that of both the Hohokam and Mogollon, sometimes resembles that of the Fremont culture. Fremont people living along the northern Colorado River drainage system in Utah may have descended from late Archaic folk of the same area who adapted some sedentary ways of the Kayenta Anasazi during Developmental Pueblo times. Their rock art includes large, deeply-engraved representations of broad-shouldered humans in ceremonial regalia, shield-bearing men, and game animals, especially bighorn sheep. It variously

39. Hohokam engraved rock art; standing figures hold hands in a frieze that resembles some painted figures on Colonial and Sedentary period pottery vessels. Original in Tucson Basin.
(After Schaafsma: 1980.)

40. Fremont style rock art, petroglyphs. Fruita Point, Capitol Reef, southern Utah. Largest figure about 5′ high.

suggests rock art of late Archaic, Basket Maker, and Developmental Pueblo eras.

The culture dates from about A.D. 900 to the thirteenth century. As was the case with many Mogollon groups, Fremont farmers were probably less sedentary than other southwestern agricultural people, relying on hunting and gathering even as they practised horticulture. Their use of ancient economic techniques supports a premise of ideological continuity suggested by similarities between their art and that of the Archaic and Basket Maker II periods. Conversely, similarities to Pueblo II art suggest that different forms of Fremont art served different, economically related ideological ends. Hieratic, large-scale images fit their Archaic traditions, worldly, small-scale art their horticultural ones. These variations also support an interpretation of Anasazi rock art that correlates its drift toward mundane subjects and human scale with increasing domestication of the Anasazi world.

That domestication did not occur in a cultural vacuum; the Anasazi were influenced by and, in turn, influenced surrounding peoples. Their culture, as was true of all of their neighbors, was shaped by a complex of physical and psychological, human, and spiritual sources and resources. From a retrospective point of view, patterns seem clear and perhaps inevitable. The Anasazi selected and rejected from a wealth of possible choices, and their decisions modified the form and direction of their culture. But apparent clarity of direction and our discovery of patterns may be historically deceptive. We know what happened, can look into the past with hindsight and offer explanations concerning its shape. But, for the most part, that shape was a consequence of a multitude of small, even trivial decisions made in their daily lives by people in search of quiet harmony, who had only the present and their own beliefs and past traditions to guide them.

Chapter Three

THE "CLASSIC PUEBLO" ANASAZI: A.D. 1000-1300

Overview of the Classic Pueblo Period

The aptly named Classic Pueblo period began in about the eleventh century and continued into the fourteenth century. It was a time of cultural florescence that overlapped with the Developmental Pueblo era and incorporated within it the latter

41. The Anasazi world during the Classic period.

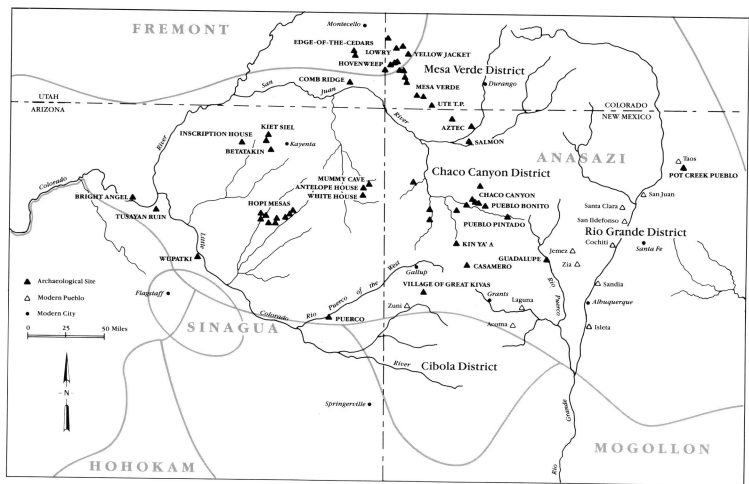

part of Pueblo II and all of Pueblo III of the Pecos Classification. Many of the most noteworthy Anasazi monuments—the great buildings of Chaco Canyon, the dramatic cliff houses of Mesa Verde, and the marvelous ruins of the Kayenta—date from this time. Those architectural achievements epitomize the era—they brought ancient Pueblo culture to the attention of nineteenth-century anthropologists, antiquarians, and historians, and their remarkable preservation continues to stimulate interest[1] in the Anasazi.

The first detailed published description of Anasazi culture was inspired by the Classic Pueblo "Great House" ruins at Chaco Canyon. These were examined in 1849 and reported upon a year later by Lt. James Simpson, a young military engineer attached to the American army. The Chaco sites were also among the first to be scientifically investigated, and studies there continue to the present. Appropriately enough, these are the earliest Classic Pueblo buildings. Many of the later but no less elaborate Classic ruins of the Mesa Verde and Kayenta also became well-known during the nineteenth century. The rock shelter towns, such as Cliff Palace at Mesa Verde and White House at Canyon de Chelly in the eastern Kayenta, are truly impressive, as are the curious, even bizarre towers of Hovenweep. But there are also larger if less spectacular sites on mesa tops and in valleys throughout the Anasazi country whose importance is only beginning to be appreciated.

South-facing rock shelters that could take advantage of solar energy during cold winters and supply shade in the very hot summers once again became favored building sites, as they had been in Basket Maker times. These are most commonly found in the Mesa Verde and Kayenta districts where there are many narrow sandstone canyons, cut by perennial streams which empty into the San Juan and Colorado Rivers. Many rock shelters are high, wide, and shallow; they encourage organization of multistoried, long, narrow, outward-facing communities. Storage buildings as well as houses at these sites are often located in dangerously high, well-protected crevices, and, where excavation into bedrock was necessary, kivas were shallow, or even built above the ground.

As in earlier times, regional variations in architecture expressed aesthetic preferences while responding to differences in local environments, materials, community size, and building functions. But the similarities from place to place are very great. In all areas, the buildings are generally compact and blocky; many are multistoried and terraced, and their aesthetic character depends upon the play of light and shadow over plane surfaces. Except in the Rio Grande drainage, where most buildings were of adobe, load-bearing walls are blocks of sandstone set in mud mortar or, in the Chaco style, more massive ones have cores of mud and stone rubble, faced on both sides by patterned veneers of finely-dressed, close-fitting

42. "Restoration of the Pueblo Hungo Pavie (Crooked Nose)." Lithograph after a watercolor by Richard H. Kern, 1849. The names for Chaco towns used by Simpson and Kern were supplied by Pueblo, Navajo, and Hispanic guides who were familiar with the Anasazi ruins. (From Simpson: 1849.)

43. Houses and storerooms in a rock crevice within a rock shelter, Grand Gulch, southeastern Utah. Pueblo III.

sandstone. Clay, adobe, or white gesso were commonly used for protective and decorative coatings on both interior and exterior surfaces, and decorative paintings were sometimes done on these, especially in the Mesa Verde region. Roofs and ceilings of earth and stone rested upon wooden rafters and small beams called *latillas*, which were set in attractive patterns. Timber was also used for posts to help support the weight of roof beams, for lintels, as horizontal stringers in stone walls, and even to support walls.

Many Classic period communities and virtually all of the Chaco style Great Houses, were initially planned or later renovated to be single, self-enclosed structures. Other towns, especially in the Mesa Verde district, were made up of a number of long buildings laid out in parallel rows. Even communities known to have grown slowly and by accretion follow these patterns. New rooms were attached side by side to older ones, creating long, parallel room blocks, or the urge to enclose space was met by adding rooms at the end of a row, which turned linear units into L shapes, Ls into Us, and Us into rectangles. If a village became old enough or grew large enough, the public space of its plaza or plazas was likely to become enclosed. Chaco plazas often held one or several Great Kivas (or ritual rooms) as well as smaller ones, those in other districts generally contained only small kivas, and small kivas were located within room blocks in all areas.

As well as kivas, most Classic period villages included forty or fewer domestic rooms that were often organized into apartments of two or three connected rooms.

107

44. A thirteenth-century wooden ceiling in a room at Spruce Tree House, Mesa Verde, Colorado. Photo by Jesse L. Nusbaum, 1907. Museum of New Mexico, Santa Fe. Clusters of small beams rest on the main cross beams and support small *latillas* and a heavy earthen floor. Note the small stones placed in the mud mortar between each masonry course to compensate for shrinkage of the mud.

45. Large timbers brought from forests at least thirty miles away are placed as stringers within the walls at Chetro Ketl in Chaco Canyon, New Mexico. Other great beams support ceilings and floors. Photographer unknown, ca. 1923. Museum of New Mexico, Santa Fe.

These were usually entered by way of a doorway facing the plaza or street or, if on an upper level, by one facing a south terrace reached by ladders leaning against lower level walls. Doorways were often rectangular, small, and had high sills. T-shaped doorways were common in Mesa Verde and some Chaco communities, and Chaco Great Houses also used corner doorways cut through the thickness of a wall. Flexible covers of matting, skins or textiles rather than hinged doors were used to cover these openings.

Upper terraces served as living areas and work spaces. Cooking fires, storage bins, floor cists, and milling basins identified kitchens and family living areas, and interior rooms were often set aside for storage. Communal work areas included open spaces or rooms in which several metates were set side-by-side; these are functionally identical to the maize-grinding rooms still found in modern pueblos, which are the focus for many social interactions. Small villages were generally less rigidly formal than larger ones and were more likely to have been built room by room over the course of the one or two generations that comprised the lifetime of most of them. Multistory communities were more common in the Chaco and Mesa Verde districts than in the Kayenta and Rio Grande areas where one-story buildings were favored. These had relatively thin walls of jacal, adobe, or blocky stone, set in masses of adobe mortar and covered with plaster.

It is obvious that Classic period town planning and construction elaborated upon procedures that had evolved during Developmental Pueblo times. And, as in the earlier period, the community networks that prospered during the Classic era were, at least in part, responses to population growth. Following a pattern that began with the origins of Anasazi culture, this growth was supported by increasingly intense agricultural exploitation of the fragile, arid environment. The earliest manifestations of the Classic period are in the southeast, in the dry Chaco district. Later, the more verdant Mesa Verde area in the north became dominant, and locally important centers developed in the arid canyonlands of the western Kayenta region and in parts of the well-watered Rio Grande valley. But, throughout the period, it seems that the Four Corners Anasazi often expanded into areas that were dangerously marginal for successful agriculture.

46. Maize-grinding room with *metates* and *manos* set side-by-side, Mesa Verde.

There were many more Anasazi communities than ever before, and many were considerably larger than those of earlier times. Some may have had as many as 5,000 or 6,000 residents; but it is more likely that the upper limit was about 3,000 and, in any event, most housed 100 people or fewer. At present, there is no secure basis for accurately estimating populations for any of the Classic period districts. The problem is complicated by several factors, among them the difficulty of judging which rooms in a community were simultaneously occupied, of knowing when villages were abandoned after brief occupations, perhaps to be reoccupied a few years later, and of recognizing seasonal homes which would have multiplied the number of residences that a family might have. Nonetheless, it may be reasonable to surmise that the many Chaco Anasazi towns housed between 15,000 and 30,000 individuals among them, and that the later Mesa Verde communities may have had twice that many people. It is likely that population densities were lower in the other Anasazi regions during the Classic period, so that the total number of people was probably on the order of 50,000 to 100,000.

Many villages were located near to each other and some, especially in the Chaco and Mesa Verde districts (but also at places such as Cedar Mesa and Black Mesa in the Kayenta area and in some valleys of the upper Rio Grande), were close enough to be considered neighborhoods of a disjunctive town rather than independent settlements. Hispanic descriptions of sixteenth-century Anasazi towns, as well as some modern-day Pueblo settlement patterns, support that interpretation, but even so it is unlikely that many such conglomerate villages housed more than a few thousand individuals. It seems that the monumental architecture of the period and the economic, social, and ritual activities that it supported would have required participation of most people living within a relatively large area, as well as commitment of a large proportion of available regional resources.

Stronger leadership and greater social stratification than were characteristic of earlier Anasazi times apparently marked the Classic period. Yet material prosperity seems to have been evenly distributed, and there is little evidence that people who lived in smaller, less impressive communities were any less well-off than those living in large and architecturally more elaborate ones. Anasazi society may have been more highly organized than in earlier days, and there were certainly more people living in a larger area, but it seems to have remained essentially egalitarian. Thus, important questions remain open regarding the motivation for building such monuments as the Chaco Great Houses and Great Kivas or the towers of Hovenweep and the other Mesa Verde communities.

Despite the material evidence for greatly increased complexity of religious, political, economic, and social systems, many of which were analogous to those of the historic pueblos, there are surprisingly few entirely original innovations. Water management systems were more sophisticated, but for the most part elaborated on earlier Anasazi methods, and, while pottery and many other arts and manufactures burgeoned, these were mainly refinements and variations upon older themes and technologies. Similarly, the elaborate calendrical and ritual concerns evidenced by solstice markers and Great Kivas had much older prototypes. Virtually all the technological and intellectual aspects of Classic Pueblo culture appear to have had their origins in earlier Anasazi practices.

In architecture, though forms might differ considerably from place to place, masonry buildings, multiroom dwellings, Great Kivas, small kivas, and plazas provided common threads that tied together Anasazi community life in all regions. Other material remains also give evidence of regional variations, sometimes quite minor, on common Anasazi themes. Cranial flattening was commonplace, and child rearing apparently was much the same all over, but infants might be bound to a

47. Fragment of reversed twill tapestry loom-woven cotton fabric from Grand Gulch, Utah. 11" x 8", Pueblo III, thirteenth century. University Museum, University of Pennsylvania.

wooden or a basketry cradle board, depending upon local custom. The dead were buried rather than cremated, usually within a village, but whether in abandoned rooms or trash middens was a matter of local choice. Farming implements including stone hoes and wooden planting sticks, and other tools, such as bows and arrows, *manos* (grinding stones) and *metates* (stone mortars), baskets, textiles, and clothing also differed only in detail in different areas.

Elsewhere in the Southwest, Anasazi styles in building, village organization, economics, ritual, and many other aspects of material and intellectual life became widespread. By the end of the period, the Anasazi had spread well beyond the upper Colorado River and Rio Grande watersheds, especially to the south where they encroached deeply into territories formerly identified with the Mogollon. Even the more distant Hohokam now showed influence of Anasazi ideas. Relationships between the Southwest and Mesoamerica may also have intensified, though the evidence for that is at best equivocal. In any event, Anasazi culture became a dominant force within the Southwest during the Classic period, and each of its major regional variants exerted great influence upon neighboring peoples.

The Chaco District: A.D. *950-1150*

Chaco Canyon is a valley located in about the middle of the 20,460 square-mile San Juan Basin, which comprises the eastern portion of the Colorado Plateau. It is in one of the more arid parts of the Southwest, about 6,000 feet above sea level, in a region of special beauty that can be searingly hot in the summer and bitterly cold in the winter. The Chaco River (or Chaco Wash) which drains it is merely an intermittent stream that feeds into the San Juan River.

People have lived in Chaco Canyon at least since the Archaic era, and it was home to Anasazi farmers from Basket Maker times. Because of its extreme aridity, it seems an unlikely place to have become the hub of a widespread cultural system that depended upon agriculture. Nonetheless, by the end of the eleventh century, hundreds of miles of roads terminated there, linking it to at least 100 related

48. The San Juan Basin, Chaco Canyon and the Chaco system of roads and outlying communities.

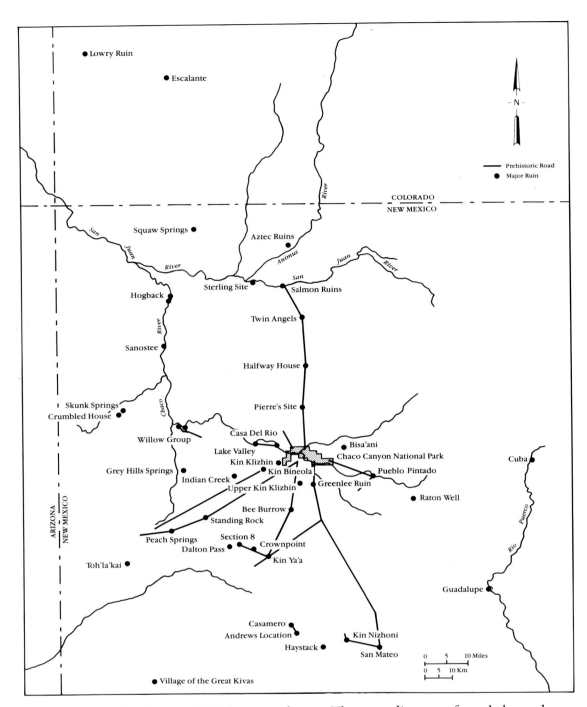

communities which we call "Chaco outliers." These outliers are found throughout the San Juan Basin, some as far as 100 miles from Chaco Canyon, and are recognized primarily by their use of the unique Chaco architectural style. Many of them predate other Classic Anasazi towns by a generation or two, while at Chaco Canyon itself the Classic period began and ended a century earlier than in other parts of the Anasazi Southwest. This widespread system of related communities is sometimes referred to as the "Chaco Phenomenon," but not all scholars agree on what is meant by that phrase.

It is generally agreed that Chaco Canyon[2] was the center of a trade network, and it may also have been a ritual center. The outliers and the roads that linked them brought a wide variety of regional goods and resources to Chaco Canyon including food, timber, turquoise, and other rare and desirable minerals. They seem also to have directed raw materials and manufactured goods from as far away as the Pacific Coast and central Mexico. Some of these materials may have been processed at

Chaco for redistribution throughout the Southwest. The Chaco Phenomenon may even be thought of as an economic and political system that was integrated and perhaps directed by religious activities centered upon the nine Great Houses and eighteen Great Kivas located within about eight miles of each other at Chaco Canyon. Some scholars have even suggested that the Chaco roads were used primarily as thruways for ritual processions and that many rooms of the Chaco Great Houses were dormitories for participants at ritual gatherings.

Architecture, especially as expressed by the Great Houses and Great Kivas, is the most characteristic material aspect of the Classic Chaco system. Chaco-style Great Houses are rectangular, circular, or D-shaped, multistoried buildings located on open sites. They were designed and built as structurally integrated units, with lower walls thicker than those above to support the weight of upper stories and set back at regulated intervals to hold the beams which supported ceilings and roofs. Their elegant geometry is expressed by the massive walls, the regular—even modular—

49. Guadalupe Ruin, a Chaco outlier along the Rio Puerco, east of Chaco Canyon. Looking northwest toward Chaco. Twelfth century.

50. The site of Grey Hills, a twelfth-century Chaco outlier investigated by National Park Service archaeologists researching the "Chaco Phenomenon."

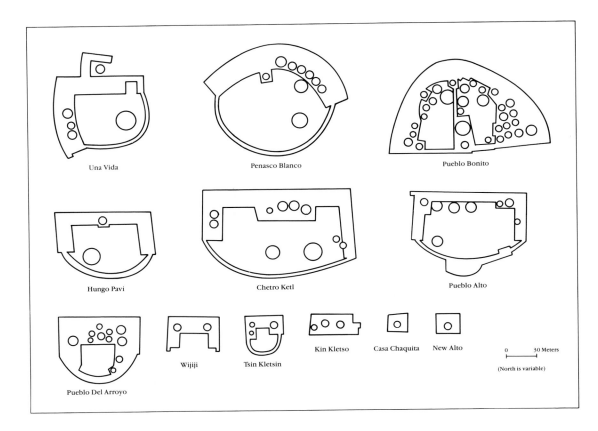

51. Simplified plan views of some Chaco Great Houses, drawn to scale.

Una Vida

Penasco Blanco

Pueblo Bonito

Hungo Pavi

Chetro Ketl

Pueblo Alto

Pueblo Del Arroyo

Wijiji

Tsin Kletsin

Kin Kletso

Casa Chaquita

New Alto

0   30 Meters

(North is variable)

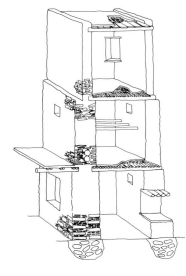

52. The Chaco method for building large, multi-storied houses. The great weight of the upper stories required massive lower walls.

proportion and size of rooms, doorways, windows, vents, niches, and other architectural details, such as the many small kivas which are perfect circles contained within rectangular rooms. The stone-rubble and mud-core load-bearing walls are encased by finely laid, decorative veneers of carefully selected sandstone, and a variety of different methods were used to lock the masonry walls together where they butted into each other.

Most Great Houses were multistoried, south-facing and terraced to maximize solar gain. Their plazas were usually walled in on the south by a one-story building unit. All the Great Houses in Chaco Canyon were on the north side of Chaco Wash and used the north wall of the canyon both as a windbreak and a solar heat collector. Their detailed planning allowed for construction by disciplined labor forces during relatively brief work episodes. Preparation activities included quarrying and dressing tons of building stone and, with human labor, hauling it several miles to a building site along with large quantities of sand, clay, and precious water needed for the adobe mix. It is estimated that 50 million pieces of sandstone were cut to build the Great House that we call Chetro Ketl.

Each Great House used hundreds or thousands of wooden beams, many of which were a foot in diameter and several yards long, for roof supports, lintels, scaffolding, and other structural needs. Wooden posts used to support the roofs of Great Kivas approached a yard in diameter, and tens of thousands of narrow poles were required for ceilings and roofs. As many as 215,000 trees went into the construction of the Great Houses and Great Kivas at Chaco. All were cut by controlled fires or with stone axes and then hand-carried to the building sites from forests that were as far away as fifty miles.

The living quarters of Chaco Great Houses were often in the form of multiroom apartment complexes. Some houses had hundreds of rooms, dozens of kivas, and several Great Kivas, which gave them the character of ceremonial centers. Many also served, at least in part, as warehouses or manufacturing centers. Pueblo Bonito, which is the both the oldest and the largest, was built in four major stages between

53. Artist's rendering of Pueblo Bonito at Chaco Canyon as it was in about 1100. Painting by Lloyd Townsend for *Readers' Digest*.

about A.D. 920 and 1120. It still stands four stories high, once had a fifth level, and contains between six hundred and eight hundred rooms and about forty kivas within the main building. Several Great Kivas are located within its huge plaza that is split in two by a long, low building. Most of the other Chaco Great Houses were built during the eleventh century, and each was somewhat different in form from any other. A few, such as Pueblo Alto and Penasco Blanco, are located on mesa tops above the canyon and adjacent to roads that connect Chaco to distant parts of the San Juan Basin.

There are many contemporaneous, smaller, more casually planned Developmental Pueblo-style villages and a few isolated Great Kivas located on the south side of the canyon floor. Similar communities and a few isolated Great Kivas are also associated with many Chaco outliers. Other than differences in architectural style, there is relatively little to distinguish the more casually planned towns from the Chaco-style communities. The social dichotomy implied by the coexistence of two such different styles of architecture is simply not supported by differences in the form and quality of other arts recovered from those places. Some quantitative differences in ritual and luxury goods lend slight support to the notion that the people who lived in the Chaco-style buildings were an elite group.

The Chacoan Great Kivas (see figure 35 on page 98) could hold hundreds of people, and those built in isolation were usually accessible to several small villages, which may have shared in their use. Regardless of location and some differences in detail, all Chaco-style Great Kivas are fundamentally similar—they were ritual theaters designed and built with the same structural elegance and superb masonry as the Great Houses. They are almost perfect circles, generally from forty-five to sixty feet across, and entered by staircases at either end of a north-south axis. Spectators could be seated on a stone bench circling the kiva floor, and some had windowed rooms on an upper level, which may have been reserved for more privileged viewers. At least one had a hidden passageway that opened under the kiva floor, presumably to allow performers to make theatrically spectacular entrances and exits. All had

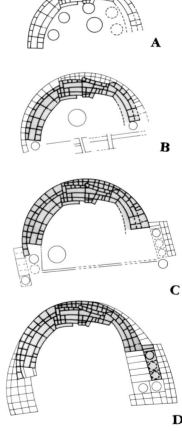

54. Construction sequence at Pueblo Bonito. A: early 900s-1020; B: 1020-1050; C: 1050-1075; D: 1075-1115. The foundation for another addition was laid but never completed. (Modified after Lekson: 1986.)

55. Excavation of the Great
Kiva at Chetro Ketl exposed
enormous sandstone disks
used as footings to hold the
four enormous posts on
which the roof rested.

stone altars, foot drums, fire boxes and fire screens. Their roofs were ordinarily
supported by four enormous wooden columns that might be cased in masonry and
rested upon yard-wide, circular stone footings sunk into the kiva floor.

Most Great Kivas were subdivided with geometric precision into two sets of
quadrants, one oriented to the cardinal directions, the other, halfway between, to
the intercardinals. Many had niches precisely spaced around the circumference.
These may have had calendric significance, and there are other relationships
between architectural details, cardinal directions, and calendrical and astronomical
regularities. These details often parallel modern Pueblo ritual patterns and· lend
support to the view that Great Kivas, like modern ones, were conceived and
designed as cosmic maps, metaphors of an ideal universe and cosmology.

The Great Houses and small villages at Chaco Canyon could conceivably have
been home to as many as 6,000 people. Chaco farmers used efficient agricultural
methods, and their water control systems, which included terraces, dams, reservoirs,
and irrigation canals, were designed to utilize all available water resources. Even so,
they could not have raised enough food for so large a group. Either the normal
population was considerably smaller than the capacity, or great quantities of food
were regularly imported from other places. The potential number of people living in
Chaco outliers was probably many times larger but, since we have no present way of
knowing if—or when—Chaco people moved from place to place within their
network, we cannot know how many of them there were.

Recent excavations suggest that the normal population at Chaco was
considerably fewer than 5,000 people. At Pueblo Alto and several other Great
Houses, comparatively few rooms were used as regular living quarters. Instead,
many were storerooms adjacent to the roads, and others, of unknown utility, lacked
fire pits and other domestic features. Rather than serving the Great House
communities, the storerooms might have had warehouselike functions, holding food
or other goods imported from one part of the Chaco network for transshipment to
another. Considering the aridity of the land and constant threat of locally
devastating droughts and other natural disasters, it may be postulated that the San
Juan Anasazi chose centrally located Chaco Canyon to be a food storage and

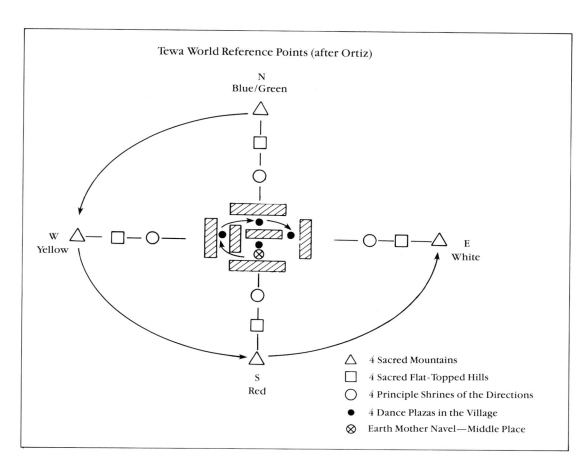

Tewa World Reference Points (after Ortiz)

N
Blue/Green

W
Yellow

E
White

S
Red

△ 4 Sacred Mountains
□ 4 Sacred Flat-Topped Hills
○ 4 Principle Shrines of the Directions
● 4 Dance Plazas in the Village
⊗ Earth Mother Navel—Middle Place

56. Landscapes that surround a Pueblo community and the kivas built within them are metaphors for the structured universe. Metaphoric details of that idealized structure are different at each Pueblo and certainly differed also among the Anasazi. (Landscape adapted from Ortiz: 1973; kiva adapted from Stirling: 1942.)

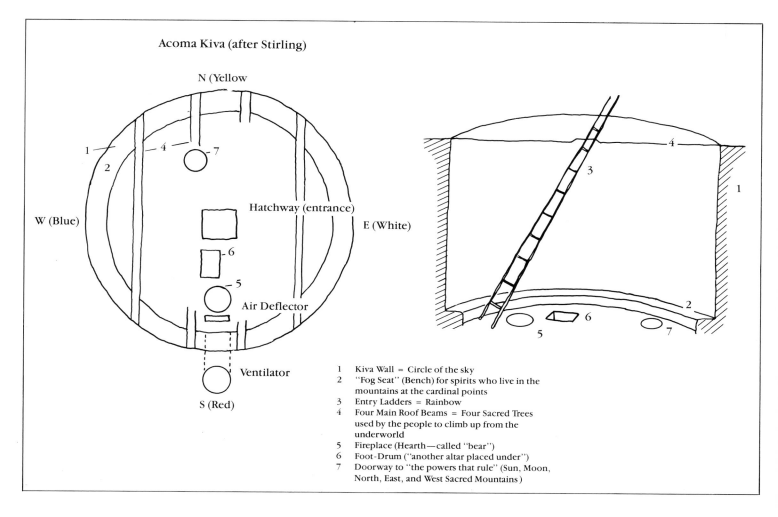

Acoma Kiva (after Stirling)

N (Yellow

W (Blue)

E (White)

Hatchway (entrance)

Air Deflector

Ventilator

S (Red)

1 Kiva Wall = Circle of the sky
2 "Fog Seat" (Bench) for spirits who live in the mountains at the cardinal points
3 Entry Ladders = Rainbow
4 Four Main Roof Beams = Four Sacred Trees used by the people to climb up from the underworld
5 Fireplace (Hearth—called "bear")
6 Foot-Drum ("another altar placed under")
7 Doorway to "the powers that rule" (Sun, Moon, North, East, and West Sacred Mountains)

57. Plan of eleventh-century garden plots ("waffle gardens") and irrigation system near Chetro Ketl which is to the north.

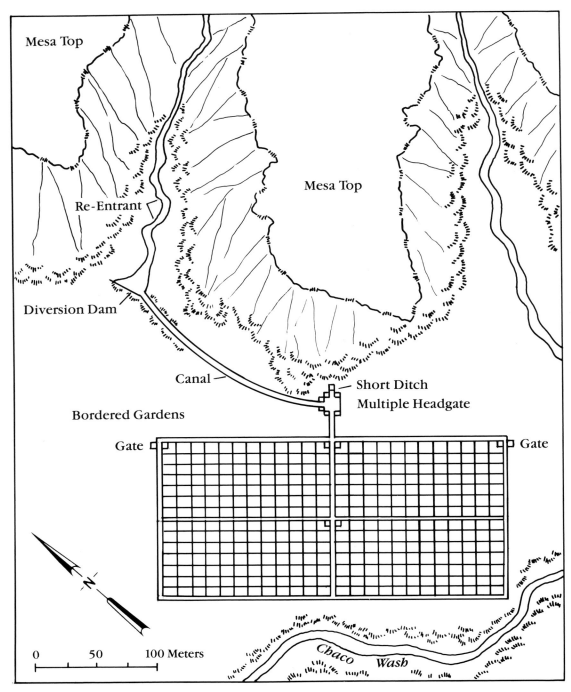

redistribution center. Adding other economic functions and ritual and political roles would have followed logically upon the original purpose.

Neither the Chaco people nor any of the other Anasazi had draft animals or wheeled vehicles, therefore the Chaco roads were built for foot traffic. Nonetheless, they are a consistent thirty feet wide for great distances, smoothly finished, curbed, and built to go directly from point to point, across valleys, mesas, and up or down cliffs on staircases cut from the sandstone. Communication between towns also utilized line-of-sight signalling stations, some of which also served as observatories and as religious shrines. Other shrines saw use as stellar or solar observatories, and it is clear that ritualists kept track of solar, lunar, and stellar cycles. Like the modern Pueblos, it appears that Chacoan priests maintained complex calendars in which the ritual and mundane spheres were fused, and practical activities such as planting were sanctioned by and invested with religious authority. That fusion of religious and secular spheres went well beyond agriculture: religion permeated the economic,

118

58. Jackson Staircase, an eleventh-century staircase behind Chetro Ketl. Photographer unknown, 1921. Museum of New Mexico, Santa Fe.

political and social ends served by the roads, the signalling stations, indeed all of the material manifestations of the Chaco Phenomenon.

We have only scattered and elusive evidence concerning the details of Chacoan ritual. Human burials are surprisingly rare, so we know very little of mortuary ceremonialism there. What we do know suggests great similarity to Anasazi customs practised elsewhere. Except for instances where ornaments of shell, jet, bone, and turquoise have been found, perhaps left as offerings, the Great Kivas have generally been bare of ritual materials. Fragments of ceremonial paraphernalia, some smashed almost beyond recognition, have been found with burials and in storage rooms at Pueblo Bonito and Chetro Ketl. These include pieces of painted wood and leather that may have been fragments of altars and ritual costumes, long, decorated flutes, and articulated, puppetlike bird and human effigies. Other effigies of pottery, stone, shell, and jet, curiously shaped implements and pottery containers, macaws (sometimes buried with great care), and copper bells from Mexico may also have

59. The so-called Sun-Dagger atop Fajada Butte marked both solstices and equinoxes. (Adapted from *National Geographic*: Nov. 1982.)

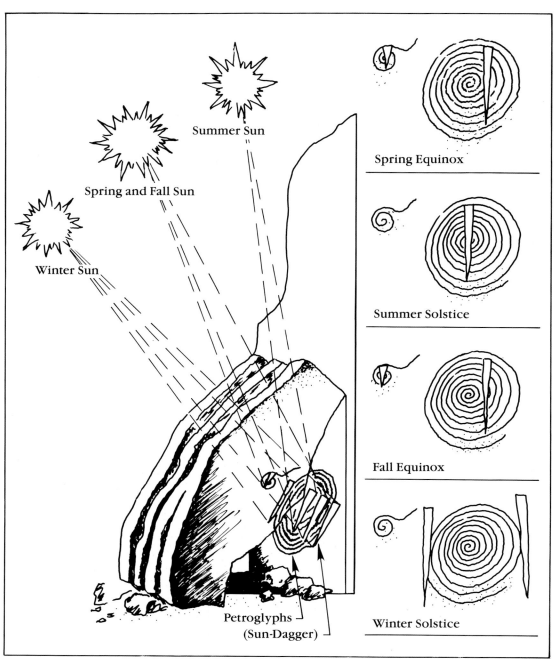

Summer Sun

Spring and Fall Sun

Winter Sun

Spring Equinox

Summer Solstice

Fall Equinox

Winter Solstice

Petroglyphs (Sun-Dagger)

60. Petroglyphs behind the Great House called Kin Kletso at Chaco Canyon, ca. eleventh century. Largest is about 28″ high.

61. Spiral and water animals are important in the rock art of the Cibola District from about the tenth century onward. Originals at the Village of the Great Kivas, a Chaco outlier near modern Zuni Pueblo in northwestern New Mexico. Largest spiral about 30″ in diameter.

had ceremonial importance. While many of these objects suggest paraphernalia used in a variety of sacred rituals by modern-day Pueblo priests, their often fragmentary nature and lack of context makes it impossible to know how any were actually used in ancient times.

There is a considerable amount of Classic period rock art at Chaco. Despite its fine quality, there is little to distinguish it from contemporary rock art made by other Anasazi people, and even such remarkable panels as the so-called Supernova near Penasco Blanco and the famous solstice markers atop Fajada Butte are not unique. The rock art apparently may refer to either the sacred or the secular, and much of it has to do with hunting. Most rock art sites are on cliff walls behind the Great Houses and in nearby side canyons so that, as elsewhere in the Anasazi world during this time, it seems to be associated with the domestic sphere.

More distinctive and precious are the remarkable turquoise, shell, and jet ornaments that might have had ceremonial value, especially those that used inlay techniques. Craftsmanship in other media, including wood, chipped stone, basketry,

62. A fragment of a painted wooden ritual object from the Chaco Canyon site of Chetro Ketl. Length 10 1/2″. National Park Service.

63. The remains of a Mexican macaw that was ritually buried at the Chaco outlier called Salmon Ruin. Twelfth century.

and pottery, can also be brilliant. And, though we know very little about textile products, we can hardly doubt that it was equal in quality. As though to stress the unity of the sacred and the secular, the patterns, motifs, and craft qualities of objects made in all of these media are virtually identical whether made for—or found in—ritual or domestic contexts. This is especially true of painted pottery which, of all arts other than architecture, is the most distinctively Chacoan. Ironically perhaps, recent evidence suggests that much of it was made at Chaco outliers rather than in Chaco Canyon proper.[3] Many painted pottery patterns are similar both in structure and detail to designs on the polychrome painted wooden and stone objects that probably served ritual functions, and to textile and basketry designs that are as old as the Basket Maker era.

Chaco pottery painting evolved from earlier, eastern Anasazi mineral-paint styles identified with the Cibola-Little Colorado tradition. It is characterized by fine, red-black lines tensely applied to a thin, chalky-white slip which covered the gray-ware vessels. Designs tended to cover most of a visible surface—bowl interiors or jar

121

64. Chaco black-on-white effigy vessel, fragment. This is a very rare realistic portrayal of an Anasazi individual. From Pueblo Bonito, ca. 1100. Ht. 6″. American Museum of Natural History, New York.

exteriors—and were likely to feature zigzag patterns of interlocking serrations. The outlined patterns were filled with closely-spaced, straight or wavy-line hatching, with solid red-black paint, or with a combination of the two. The dominant tonal effect is of shades of gray, which modify the angular tensions of the painted designs. The wares tend to be thin, hard, and durable.

Large, painted storage jars have high shoulders, small mouths, and a low center of gravity; their patterns are best perceived from above, suggesting that their usual placement was on the floor of a room. They differ in form, as well as decoration, from the more common unpainted vessels that were made for storage or cooking and are usually wide-mouthed, bag-shaped, and elaborately decorated with fine-scaled, corrugated textures. Other painted forms include round-bodied, high-necked vessels with side handles, which may have been used as drinking containers, scoops, ladles, and several sizes of shallow bowl, presumably for food service. Among unusual shapes, the most notable are tall cylinder vases, lobed jars, and effigy vessels. As well as pottery from the outliers, other painted trade wares from the Mesa Verde, Kayenta, and Mogollon border regions are also commonly found.

Elsewhere in the Southwest during the time of the Chaco florescence and continuing through the remainder of the post-Chacoan Classic period, similar high levels of craft production are in evidence. But it is architecture, roads, and the social, political, economic, and ritual implications of these grand material accomplishments which set Chaco apart most emphatically from the rest of the Anasazi until the twelfth century. The elaboration of Anasazi architecture, which began late in the tenth century, spread during the eleventh century, and reached its climax before A.D. 1130. For reasons that are not yet clear, the Chaco system ended by about A.D. 1150.

At Chaco Canyon and at some Chaco outliers, Great Houses were occupied and sometimes remodelled during the thirteenth century by people who used Mesa Verdean-style architecture, pottery, and ritualism. The Great House of Kin Kletso at

65. Exotic Mesa Verde canteen from Pueblo Bonito in Chaco Canyon. McElmo black-on-white, ca. 1100. School of American Research Collections at the Museum of New Mexico, Santa Fe.

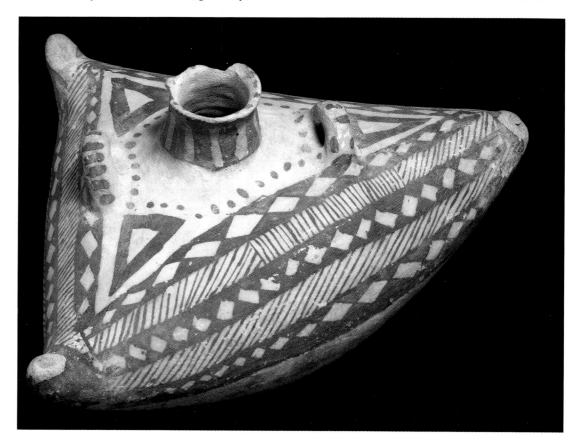

Chaco, and at least one unit of the enormous Chaco outlier that we call Aztec Ruin, are Mesa Verdean rather than Chacoan in style. It is an open question whether these were built by Chaco people or by migrants from the Mesa Verde, but regardless, the Chaco era was over. Well before A.D. 1300, Chaco Canyon was abandoned, never again to be home to an Anasazi people. During the remainder of the Classic Pueblo era, Anasazi culture centered in the Mesa Verde and Kayenta regions.

The Mesa Verde District: A.D. *1100-1300*

The areas north and west of Chaco Canyon were occupied by many Anasazi people all during the time of the Chaco Phenomenon. For the most part, they lived on mesa tops or in valleys in relatively small, Pueblo II style communities similar in many respects to the contemporary small towns found along the south side of Chaco Canyon. Whether built of masonry, adobe, or jacal, these ordinarily included a few domestic suites of two or three connected rooms and one or two small kivas located

66. Inaccessible House, a small Pueblo III cliff house under the escarpment at Mesa Verde. Photo by Jesse L. Nusbaum, 1907. Museum of New Mexico, Santa Fe.

within or in front of a room block.

These northern and western Anasazi were certainly aware of the Chaco system, and those living on the periphery of the San Juan Basin even participated in it to some extent. Pottery and other goods were exchanged with Chaco, Chaco outliers such as the Lowry Ruin were located in the very heart of the Mesa Verde country and, by 1100, Mesa Verde style kivas, domestic buildings, and other architectural elements were in use at Chaco communities. Chacoan architecture was also influential in the eastern Kayenta at places such as the White House Ruin at Canyon de Chelly. But the levels of regional interaction and centralization that identify the Chaco system with the Classic Pueblo era seem not to have been reached elsewhere in the Anasazi world until near the end of the Chaco florescence and were never achieved in many places, even then.

Nonetheless, there was a considerable degree of localized complexity during Pueblo II times in many parts of the Anasazi southwest. This was especially true of the Mesa Verde district, which extends from southwestern Colorado to southeastern Utah, and includes the green tablelands of Mesa Verde National Park, the Montezuma Valley and other equally verdant valleys northwest and west of Mesa Verde, and the considerably more arid Hovenweep country to the west. It is a high country, 6,300 feet above sea level in the Montezuma Valley, and more than 600 feet above that on the Mesa Verde escarpment. Even though the short, frost-free growing season makes it marginal for growing maize, it is attractive to farmers during warm cycles because it gets considerably more moisture than most other parts of the Southwest—about fourteen inches in a normal year as compared to less than half that at Chaco Canyon.[4]

Anglo-American farmers and ranchers who settled there late in the nineteenth century plowed over and looted many Anasazi sites. But some among them, including Richard Wetherill and his brothers, who explored the Mesa Verde cliff

67. The Far View Community at Mesa Verde, ca. twelfth century. House units were located within fields bounded by two irrigation canals fed from the reservoir that we call Mummy Lake. (After National Park Service.)

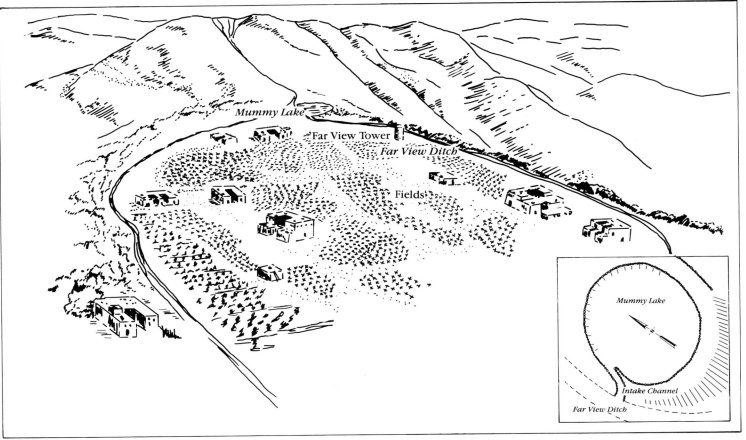

houses, brought the antiquities to the attention of scholars and the public, and many of these ruins were ultimately protected.

The Mesa Verde Anasazi are best known for the spectacular, late Classic period masonry cliff houses found just below the Mesa Verde escarpment. They are enclosed by the rock shelters in which they were built, and this framing as well as their fundamental geometry, are basic points of similarity to the Chaco Great Houses. But, unlike the carefully planned Great Houses, which are artificially enclosed on open building sites, the cliff houses are clusters of separate structures joined together, stacked vertically, and stepped back to fill three-dimensional, naturally concave spaces. Unlike the massive yet delicate Chaco masonry, Mesa Verde walls are generally only one or two stones thick and made of large, carefully shaped, bricklike blocks of sandstone. They were often coated with plaster and sometimes decorated with monochromatic paintings. The cliff houses use a greater variety of geometric forms, including cylindrical and rectangular towers, and their complex spontaneity is in sharp contrast with the stately rationality of Chaco Great Houses.

But, for all the expressive power of the cliff houses, it was the high mesa tops and the valleys below that were the loci of Mesa Verde cultural elaboration during late Developmental and Classic Pueblo times. For example, the Far View Community[5] on Chapin Mesa in Mesa Verde National Park was begun during the 900s and, by 1100, had grown to include eighteen Pueblo II style villages with a total population of about 500. Each village had one or two small, circular kivas, perhaps used by kin groups, that are typically Mesa Verde in style, with a bench and six evenly-spaced pilasters supporting a dome-shaped crib roof. The villages shared use of a stone-lined reservoir (called Mummy Lake today), built in the tenth century, which could hold almost two million gallons of water.

They built no large houses or central ceremonial places until after 1100, but Mummy Lake was one of several public works which unified the Far View villages into a single community. Less visible today are many agricultural terraces and an irrigation canal system several miles long, which directed water to the reservoir as well as to the fields. These were also shared by all of the villages, and it seems that access to the field system provided the logic for their settlement pattern.

By about 1100, a move toward centralization was begun with construction of several relatively large, compact buildings, similar in plan but different in many structural and formal details from Chaco-style Great Houses. The largest of these is called Far View House, and it once stood three stories high and had about fifty rooms and five kivas, including one that approaches the size[6] of a Great Kiva. Though some walls had rubble cores, the blocky masonry is identical with that of the later cliff houses. Their T-shaped doorways and keyhole kivas, with benches and pilasters, are also typical of Classic Mesa Verde architecture.

Other of the new-style villages have stone towers, believed to be ceremonial buildings, some of which are connected to kivas by way of hidden tunnels. Collectively, these buildings demonstrate the new emphasis that was placed on centralizing institutions early in the twelfth century; they define the beginnings of the local Classic Pueblo period.

By 1200, the Far View Community was abandoned, and its people had moved some six miles south to build new homes in rock shelters 300 to 600 feet below the mesa top. Among these is the largest of the Mesa Verde cliff houses, Cliff Palace, which has 220 rooms, 23 kivas, and housed between 250 and 350 people. But cliff houses generally are no larger than the old, mesa-top villages. Some large buildings constructed on mesa tops at about the same time, including the one we now call Sun Temple, seem to have been used as ritual centers serving the cliff house towns.

68. Kiva, Far View House, Mesa Verde. Its large size (about 25' across) and features such as the massive stone deflector and the stone-lined foot drums suggest Chaco Great Kivas. Continuity with earlier Mesa Verde kiva traditions is even more evident. ca. 1100.

Meanwhile, the irrigation canals and other waterworks were extended to serve the new and more complex towns. These serve to remind us that the centralizing innovations which define the Mesa Verde Classic Period depended upon public works produced by integrative socio-economic systems that were three centuries old.

The evolution of the Far View Community is typical of many locations both on the Mesa Verde escarpment and in neighboring valleys and mesas. The population of the highland settlements probably never exceeded 2,500 or 3,000, and it seems that the heaviest concentrations of Mesa Verde people, perhaps as many as 30,000, were in the valleys that drain into the Dolores River to the north, and along the edge of the mesas that overlook McElmo and Mancos Canyons to the west.

Systematic investigation of the many small villages and large towns of those areas has only begun.[7] It now appears that the largest of them have many hundreds of residential rooms and numerous kivas, towers, and other ritual structures. Some, for example, Yellow Jacket, located in a broad valley, are organized as agglomerations of linear room blocks, laid out in parallel streets. Yellow Jacket is more than one-half mile long and might have had 100 kivas, including at least one Great Kiva, as well as towers, shrines, and other ceremonial spaces. It is not yet clear if it was a ritual center, a town of 3,000 or more people, or both.

Other large communities, such as those on mesa edges at Sand Canyon and Goodman Point, are on rolling, tree-covered sites that isolate the building clusters into distinct neighborhoods and disguise their configurations. Though many are considerably larger than any of the Mesa Verde cliff houses, none of these ruins are as well-preserved or as visually powerful. And, though they are as large or larger than any of the Chaco towns, none have the massive architectural presence of the Chaco Great Houses. They are so disturbed or have sunk so deeply into the landscape that whatever architectural character they may once have had is now hidden or lost entirely.

Other Classic period Mesa Verde settlements were located further west, in the more arid Hovenweep country. Rather than in large centralized towns, Hovenweep

70. Yellow Jacket in the Montezuma Valley, Colorado. One of the largest Pueblo III Anasazi sites known.

126

people lived in relatively small building clusters, located near spring-fed streams that ran for short distances in narrow, shallow canyons. Groups of them built homes at the head of a canyon, along its rim, on great boulders within it, and, occasionally, in rock shelters above the canyon floor. These were truly oasis communities in which as many as 500 people might live in groups of just a few families each, located within one-half mile of each other. They corporately constructed and maintained extensive water control systems that not only utilized the springs that seem to have been essential to them, but also built dams, canals, and reservoirs to collect rainfall coming off the slick-rock mesa tops. Canals also directed agricultural water toward their terraced or walled fields and to alluvial areas where sand was used as a water-preserving mulch.

They appear not to have built any large-scale, ceremonial structures but had many small kivas and towers. The towers are often isolated on top of free-standing boulders and are shaped to fit the contours of the natural sandstone formations. They tend to be high, as though growing out of the rock, and their massive, blank walls of honey-colored sandstone blocks are broken only by a few rectangular openings. Their clean, sculptural qualities, and the illusion that they fuse with the native rock, give them an extraordinary visual power—they are artistic statements expressive of the continuity of culture and nature.

As was the case at Chaco Canyon, we have little detailed knowledge of Mesa Verde ritualism, but the formality and pomp suggested by the architectural monuments of Chaco, especially the Great Kivas, seems not to be present. Kivas tended to be small—not even the large ones were very elaborate—and most were hardly visible, for their domed roofs were flat on top and actually supported the open spaces of small plazas where public rituals may have been held. And, even if places such as Yellow Jacket prove to have been ritual centers, the scattered nature of their site plans, without a single great plaza or any large, dominating structure, argues against their ever having had a Chaco-like monumentality.

In other respects also, Mesa Verde ritualism seems to have been different in character. The monochromatic paintings sometimes found on kiva walls are usually

73. Mesa Verde-style petroglyphs, Grand Gulch, southeastern Utah, ca. thirteenth century. Largest figure about 11″ high.

74. Pottery bowl, Mesa Verde black-on-white. The overall design of interlocking spirals is unusual. Diameter 7 ¹/₂″. Thirteenth century, University Museum, University of Pennsylvania.

Opposite:

54. Aerial view of Chaco Canyon looking southwest, New Mexico. The Great Houses of Chetro Ketl (lower left), and Pueblo Bonito (far right) are visible. Tenth to twelfth centuries.

Following pages:

55. The Tower Kiva of Chetro Ketl, Chaco Canyon. Eleventh century.

geometric, but some paintings, as well as rare engravings on kiva floors, are of ithyphallic, humpbacked flute players, personages who were prominent in rock art throughout the Anasazi Southwest. These are supernaturals, probably associated with both fertility and hunting, which was an important economic activity throughout the Mesa Verde country. Their appearance in kivas suggests analogy with hunting society rituals of modern Rio Grande Pueblos in kivas that serve small-scale fraternal, religious, and curing organizations. Mesa Verde rock art likewise tended to be small-scale, and panels are often loaded with images of hunting and domestic scenes, animals, and supernaturals.

There is ample evidence throughout the Mesa Verde region that solar and stellar observations were regularly made, presumably by priests, to maintain calendars for regulating both economic and ritual affairs. These fusions of the sacred and the secular, and of nature and culture, were expressed in many material ways. The same decorative forms that appear on domestic textiles, baskets, and pottery were also painted on the walls of kivas, which might take on the appearance of enormous painted pottery bowls as though there were no conceptual distinction between a pottery container and a kiva wall.

Motifs and design structures used on Mesa Verde painted pottery may be similar to those used on Chaco wares, but artistic treatment was quite different in each tradition. Figure-ground inversions that create ambiguous, positive-negative patterns became commonplace on Mesa Verde pottery after about 1000 and continued through the Classic period. Smoothly painted, broad black lines on polished white slips, which might have a satin sheen, characterize the style which is in strong contrast to the tense, angular, fine-line hatching and gray tones of the Chaco tradition. Intermediate grays made by hachuring are uncommon, replaced by equally weighted contrasted masses of dark and light. By 1200, craftsmanship was uniformly superb and some potters may have identified their work with hallmarks.[8]

During the course of the thirteenth century, occasional droughts adversely affected different areas of the Mesa Verde district, in some cases for several consecutive years, but there seems to have been no severe, lengthy drought that affected all of the region at the same time. During the same period, there may have

56. *Overview of Cliff Palace,*
Mesa Verde, Colorado.

Following pages:

57. *Cliff Palace, Mesa Verde.*
Thirteenth century.

58. *Overview of Antelope*
House, Canyon de Chelly,
Kayenta District, Arizona.

59. *Antelope House, Canyon*
de Chelly. The masonry of
eastern Kayenta buildings
tends to be finer and more
elaborate than that of the
western Kayenta region.
Eleventh to thirteenth
centuries.

60. An ancient wooden ceiling preserved at Pueblo Bonito, Chaco Canyon, northwestern New Mexico. ca. 1100.

61. Interior of Pueblo del Arroyo, Chaco Canyon. Note original roof beams and other structural details. ca. 1075-1115.

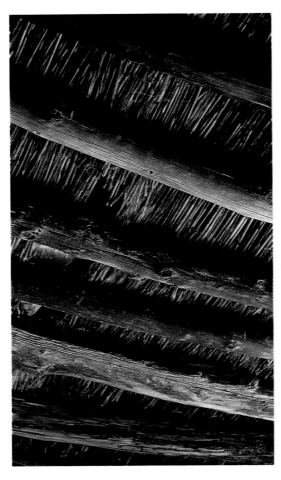 

62. 63. Doorways within Pueblo Bonito, Chaco Canyon. Upper floors have fallen in here so that upper doorways (including the high corner doorway) look like high windows. ca. 1100.

64. Milling basins for grinding corn, made in a sandstone boulder at a village in a rock shelter in Grand Gulch, southeastern Utah. Pueblo III.

65. Wooden hoes and digging sticks used to plant and cultivate maize. A stone hoe would have been hafted to the shaft second from left. Longest ca. 55". ca. 900-1100. National Park Service, Chaco Canyon.

66. Coiled basket of natural and dyed fibers. Ht. 10". Cibola region. Thirteenth century. Chamber of Commerce Museum, Grants, New Mexico.

67. Pueblo Bonito from the air, looking north. Chaco Canyon, New Mexico. Note the rock fall which destroyed portions of the town in 1941. Tenth to twelfth centuries.

68. 69. Great Kiva (opposite, left) and kiva (opposite, right), Pueblo Bonito.

70. Overview of Pueblo Bonito.

71. A suite of ground floor rooms of Pueblo Bonito at Chaco Canyon used modular doorways. ca. 1100.

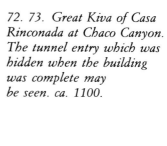

72. 73. Great Kiva of Casa Rinconada at Chaco Canyon. The tunnel entry which was hidden when the building was complete may be seen. ca. 1100.

Following pages:

74. An alley-like ground-floor passageway at Chetro Ketl, Chaco Canyon. ca. 1100.

75. Tower kiva and signalling station at the Chaco outlier called Kin Ya'a, New Mexico. ca. 1100.

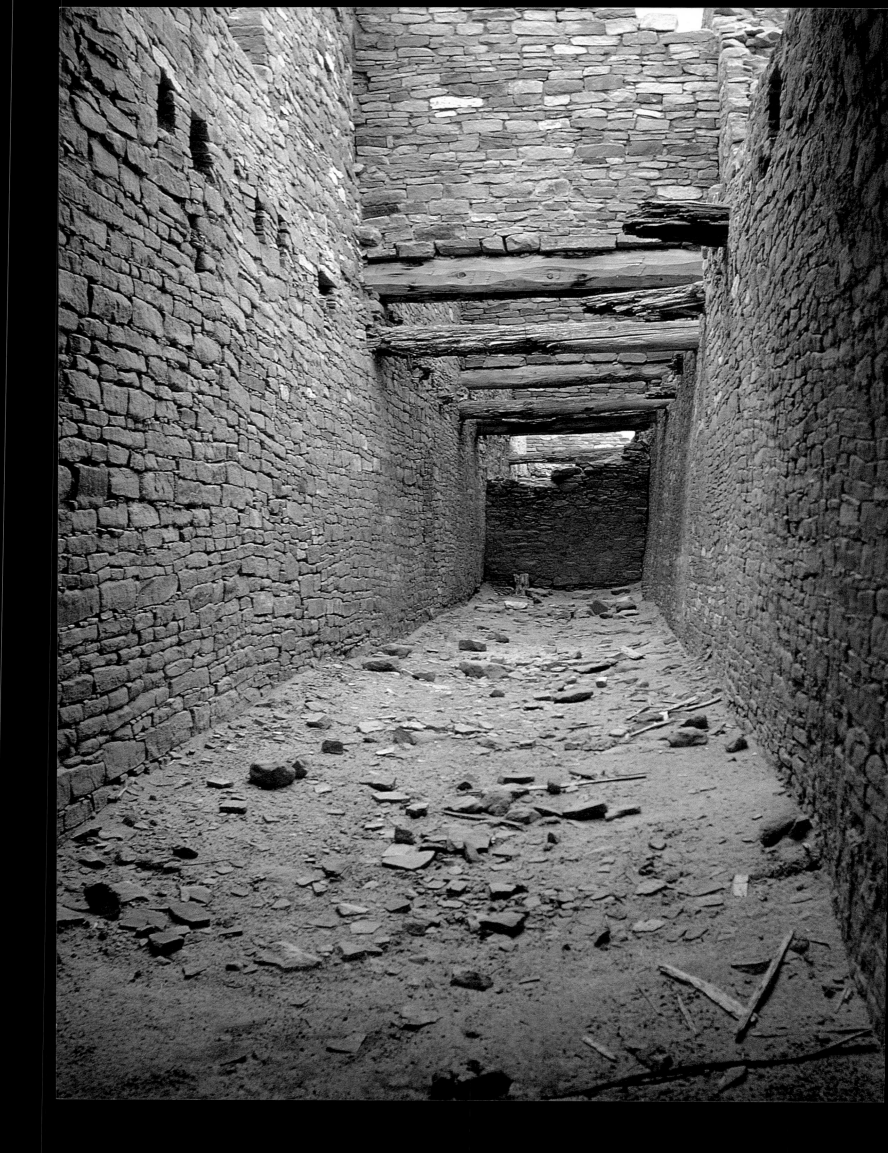

76. Fajada Butte looms over
the south entrance to Chaco
Canyon in the early morning
mist. The so-called Sun-
Dagger is atop this mountain.

Opposite:

77. The so-called Sun-Dagger
petroglyph atop Fajada Butte
in May, 1985.

78. *Chacoan Great Kiva at the large Chaco outlier called Aztec, northwestern New Mexico. (Reconstructed.)*

79. *Great Kiva, Aztec, inside view.*

Opposite:

80. *Great Kiva, Aztec. Access to one of the fourteen small rooms encircling the kiva.*

Following pages:

81. *Elaborate shell and jet necklaces and many pieces of worked turquoise were deposited in the closed niches that line the wall of the Great Kiva at Chetro Ketl, Chaco Canyon. Eleventh century. School of American Research Collections at the Museum of New Mexico, Santa Fe.*

82. 83. *Gallup black-on-white olla, probably for carrying water. Side view, ht. 20". Top view, diameter 17". Eleventh century. Note resemblance to bowl designs in plate 19. Laboratory of Anthropology, Museum of New Mexico, Santa Fe.*

84. *From right: a basketry tube covered with bits of turquoise, a bone instrument inlaid with turquoise and jet, and a fine McElmo black-on-white drinking mug from Mesa Verde were recovered by the Pepper-Wetherill excavations at Pueblo Bonito, Chaco Canyon, in 1896. Tube ht. 7 ¹/₂". Eleventh century. American Museum of Natural History, New York.*

85. *Three pottery vessels recovered from excavations at Chaco Canyon. From left: small boot-shaped jar with animal (skunk or badger) handle, Gallup black-on-white; bird-shaped jar, Escavada black-on-white; gourd-shaped ladle, Chaco black-on-white. Ladle is 11" long. Late eleventh century. School of American Research Collection at the Museum of New Mexico, Santa Fe.*

88. *Cliff Palace, Mesa Verde. Monochromatic painting high up in a tower. The lower floors have fallen in.*

89. *Cliff Palace, Mesa Verde. In this cliff dwelling, walls are made of large, carefully shaped, brick-like blocks of sandstone.*

90. *Far View House, one of several large, compact apartment style houses built at Mesa Verde in about 1100.*

91. *Sun Temple at Mesa Verde seems to have been an elaborate and complex ritual structure that was contemporaneous with the thirteenth-century cliff houses at Mesa Verde.*

92. *Far View Tower, a ritual structure associated with a small kiva was a part of the large, multi-unit Far View community. Similar towers are found at other Mesa Verde sites.*

*93. 94. Small, highly stylized
kivas at Far View House,
Mesa Verde. ca. 1100.*

95. Kiva at Far View
House, Mesa Verde.

96. Sun Temple,
Mesa Verde.

Following Pages:

97. Kiva at Lowry Ruin with
painted banquette that uses a
Mesa Verde pottery design.
Twelfth century. The Lowry
Ruin is west and north of the
Mesa Verde escarpment and
is thought to be a Chaco
outlier.

98. Betatakin, a late
thirteenth-century western
Kayenta village in Tsegi
Canyon, northern Arizona. It
is located within a
spectacularly large rock
shelter that offers shade and
protection from rain in the
summers and allows the
warm, low-lying winter sun
to penetrate deeply into it.

99. Antelope House Ruin,
Canyon de Chelly, eastern
Kayenta District, Arizona.
Eleventh to thirteenth
centuries.

100. Mesa Verde and Kayenta pottery. The canteen, ladle, and mug are all thirteenth-century Mesa Verde black-on-white wares. The bowl, from northern Arizona is a twelfth-century eastern Kayenta type. Canteen is 5" high, ladle is 9 ³/₄" long. Indian Art Fund, School of American Research, Santa Fe.

101. 102. Two views of the White House Ruin, Canyon de Chelly eastern Kayenta District, Arizona. Right: the multi-storied ruin at the base of the cliff resembles a Chacoan outlier. The very large lizard figure on the cliff wall is visible from a great distance. Eleventh to thirteenth centuries.

103. Wupatki, a Sinagua
site dating from ca. 1120 to 1210
built near the volcanic cinder
cones and cinder fields of
Sunset Crater in northern
Arizona. The walled
but unroofed structure
in the foreground is
thought to have been
a dance court.

104. *Pottery bowl, Mimbres black-on-white, southwestern New Mexico. The tense linearity, fine lines, and use of hachuring as well as black-on-white coloration evidences the strength of Anasazi influence upon the pottery of this southern Mogollon group. Ht. 5". ca. 1100. Maxwell Museum of Anthropology, Albuquerque.*

105. *Pottery bowl, St. John's polychrome, west-central New Mexico and east-central Arizona. Similar designs were made in the same Mogollon region on Anasazi-like white wares. The shiny glaze paint, development of a design field on the exterior, and the use of black paint on a red slip prefigures Anasazi glaze-painted wares of the Pueblo IV period. Ht. 5 3/4". ca. 1275-1300, Laboratory of Anthropology, Museum of New Mexico, Santa Fe.*

been raids and other incursions by invading groups of nomadic peoples, but the evidence is scant for that. Whatever the cause or causes, Mesa Verde people began to migrate southward toward the Rio Grande Valley during the last quarter of the century, and by about 1300 they had abandoned their country entirely. In some instances, there is evidence of violence and, in a few cases, it appears that a town was abandoned in haste with many possessions left behind. But most often the evidence points to an orderly and peaceful migration[9] whose causes remain undiscovered.

Opposite:

106. Montezuma Castle, a Sinagua site in the Verde Valley below the Mogollon Rim, north-central Arizona. Late thirteenth century.

The Kayenta District: A.D. 1100-1300

Westward of Hovenweep, in Grand Gulch and other canyons that drain into the San Juan River, there are many ruins of small Classic Pueblo communities that share characteristics of both the Mesa Verde and the Kayenta districts. Those canyons at the northern edge of the Kayenta district also border upon the marginally agricultural Fremont people. During the Classic period, the Kayenta District in northeastern Arizona was between the Grand Canyon on the west and Canyon de Chelly on the east, and it extended southward to the Mogollon Rim.

Precipitation may be plentiful anywhere in that region at elevations above 7,200 feet, but below that the land is dry. Its high mesas are cut by sometimes deep and often spectacular canyons; and monolithic volcanic outcrops, cinder cones, volcanic dikes, and saw-toothed ridges punctuate the fantastic landscape. Portions of it were occupied by Anasazi people from earliest Basket Maker times, but population density was never high and few places were lived in for more than two or three consecutive generations. Late in the Classic period, Tsegi Canyon, Canyon de Chelly, and the southern end of Black Mesa were the population centers, but it is unlikely that many more than 2,000 people ever lived in any of those places at one time.

The high mesa tops could only be farmed during brief and unpredictable warm cycles, and arable land in the sometimes more temperate canyon bottoms was at a premium and subject to the vagaries of rainfall and shallow springs. Rock shelters

75. Split Level Ruin, Grand Gulch, southeastern Utah. The roof of a kiva is visible at lower left. Remains of Basket Maker sites are usually found in the same rock shelters where the thirteenth-century villages were built.

76. White House Ruins in Canyon de Chelly, Arizona. Photo by Timothy H. O'Sullivan, 1873. Museum of New Mexico, Santa Fe. This is among the earliest photographs of Anasazi ruins.

77. Antelope House, detail. Canyon de Chelly, Arizona.

above the precious fields were favored building sites, and the great cliff houses of Betatakin and Keet Seel in Tsegi Canyon are typical of Classic period Kayenta architecture except for their relatively large size. They combine masonry and jacal walls, their building stones are trimmed but not cleanly dressed, and their stone walls are usually only one block thick and set in a great deal of mud mortar. Compared to Mesa Verde and Chaco architecture, these are simple structures. But they are now also two of the best preserved Anasazi ruins anywhere, and lovely in their impressive settings.

Both cliff houses were built during the 1270s and abandoned by about 1300. Neither housed more than about 125 to 150 people, who presumably had lived on nearby mesa tops in earlier times. They were both built during the course of only a few years and are nicely unified but, unlike Mesa Verde cliff houses, they are dominated by domestic structures. There are multiroom apartment houses and community work areas, but no towers and only a few kivas, which are small, square, sunk into small plazas, and virtually invisible from a distance. There seem to be no large ritual or ceremonial structures or spaces of any kind.

Perhaps 500 other people lived in Tsegi Canyon in similar but smaller villages, located within ten miles of either large cliff house. Each appears to have been entirely autonomous, with little evidence of regional, cooperative structures such as the reservoirs and canals that are typical of the Chaco and Mesa Verde districts. These Kayenta people were organized into small, flexible social units. Fremont-like, they invested less in their buildings than did other Classic period Anasazi, and, unlike most others, left a fair amount of evidence that warfare and defense were important considerations in their lives.

Canyon de Chelly (like Tsegi Canyon, this is an English language corruption of the Navajo word *tseqi* meaning "rock canyon") and its northern arm, called Canyon del Muerto, is wider, better watered, and has more arable land than most other Kayenta site locations. For those reasons, it seems to have been continuously occupied for longer periods of time. Basket Maker villages underlie most of the Classic Pueblo ones, and some of the latter were begun during the Developmental

Pueblo era. Proximity to both Chaco and Mesa Verde left influences here. Walls built at White House during the eleventh century have a Chaco character, and those built in the thirteenth century at Mummy Cave are Mesa Verdean. White House seems to have been continuously occupied for about 250 years, and Antelope House—which has much more typical Kayenta-style masonry—for almost that long. Yet the total population of those two great canyons may never have exceeded 1,000, and none of the ruins was as large as either Keet Seel or Betatakin.

As happened throughout the Four Corners during the thirteenth century, most of the Kayenta territory was abandoned by about 1300, with many people withdrawing to the Hopi Mesas at the southern end of Black Mesa. A combination of environmental and human factors may explain the abandonment of this territory. The periodic droughts toward the end of the thirteenth century probably caused more stress here than elsewhere, for it is country that is normally too arid to long resist any kind of drought and too fragile to resist the impact of farming peoples. Lowered water tables in the narrow canyons made once arable land unsuitable for agriculture, while the thin soils were washed away, and the canyons cut by arroyos when they were cleared of trees and other natural ground cover so that crops could be planted. Poor crops, the threat of famine, and raiding neighbors may explain the defensive character of late Classic Kayenta towns and the occasional violence uncovered by modern archaeologists.

Population density had always been considerably lower in the Kayenta region than in the other major Anasazi districts, and the region has a rustic flavor. Architecture was simpler, and ritual and social institutions also appear to have been less complex. Rock art tends to be somewhat larger in scale, less diverse, and places greater emphasis on animal figures then is seen in the other regions; the art also has a somewhat Archaic flavor. But in some respects, for example, in their painted pottery and perhaps their textile arts, the Kayenta people show more, rather than less complexity than the Anasazi of other regions. Color was an important element in both of these arts, as was use of complex, interlocking fourfold patterns that rotate about a square center.

Most painted pottery was black-on-white, carbon-painted ware similar to that of

78. Kayenta pictographs from the site of Betatakin, late thirteenth century. The shield is about 45″ in diameter. The shield painting is tan on white, all others are white only.

79. Black painted cotton textile from Hidden House, central Arizona, thirteenth century. Original is 64″ long. Associated with the Sinagua culture it shows the interaction between western Anasazi (Kayenta) and Hohokam decorative practices.

80. Kayenta-style one-handled pottery bowl from northern Arizona, south of Black Mesa. It has a negative design of interlocking scrolls. Walnut black-on-white. Ht. 5″. Early twelfth century. Laboratory of Anthropology, Museum of New Mexico, Santa Fe.

81. Kayenta-style one-handled pottery bowl from Betatakin at the northern end of Black Mesa. Kayenta polychrome. Ht. 4 ½". Late twelfth century. Indian Art Fund, School of American Research.

Mesa Verde but more likely to use rotating designs, overall patterns, and designs that expand or contract as though the paint were a flexible film placed over an expanding and contracting bulbous form. Paint and slip may be highly polished and almost luminescent, and black dominates, so much so that an unpainted, pearly-white slip may give the illusion of being a painted, white line on a black surface. Orange-slipped and polychrome wares were made, similar in form and pattern to black-on-white pottery, but their colors add a bright complexity and another qualitative dimension.

Shapes of the Classic Kayenta pottery tradition are refined: bowls are deep; jars may be deep bowls covered by flat upper shoulders and pierced by delicately raised rims; ollas are round or ovate with tiny openings. Considering the provincial character of the Kayenta region, their pottery is surprisingly diverse and sophisticated. Perhaps, not so surprisingly, it was widely distributed and had a long-lasting impact on later Anasazi pottery traditions.

Anasazi Neighbors: A.D. 1000-1300

The Anasazi florescence of the tenth through thirteenth centuries has sometimes been attributed to intensified relationships between the Southwest and Mesoamerica. Trade guilds, operating from several Mesoamerican centers during those centuries, organized long-range expeditions, and it is surmised that some of these may have come as far north as the Southwest. Members of these guilds sometimes controlled the trade in foreign regions by establishing collection and redistribution centers for regional manufactures and raw materials. They also encouraged trade in the areas that came under their influence by helping to organize economic and social trading institutions and mechanisms.

The ruins of Casas Grandes[10] in northern Chihuahua, dating from the eleventh through the middle of the fourteenth century, have the character of a Mesoamerican trade center, including strong similarities to Mesoamerican house and town planning, and public and ritual architecture. But there is no evidence of any profound Mesoamerican influence on the Classic period Anasazi that came from there—or anywhere else for that matter. Interactions between Casas Grandes and the more northerly parts of the Southwest certainly occurred before 1300, but there are no obvious ritual, public, or domestic architectural influences, and none on pottery design or technology. Casas Grandes was hardly instrumental in shaping the Classic period Anasazi, and it seems likely that most interactions between the two regions were either indirect or casual. It may have been that Casas Grandes was headquarters to a handful of Mesoamerican traders who systematically gathered goods from all over the vast northwestern frontier of Middle America for shipment south. If so, the Anasazi Southwest, at the very northern limits of their territory, could not have engaged much of their physical attention. Conversely, Anasazi influences during those centuries seem to have moved southward.

Before the tenth century, innovations and elaborations of southwestern cultures tended to start in the south and move northward to Anasazi territory. The Anasazi modified new ideas and patterned them to conform to one or another variant of a generic Anasazi style. During the tenth century and later, as Anasazi communities grew in size and complexity, their economic and social networks expanded, and the direction of cultural influences within the Southwest was reversed. Many of the more northerly Mogollon and Hohokam communities, as well as cultures that were less widespread or not so well known, began to take on an Anasazi character. By the twelfth century, Anasazi styles in architecture, pottery decoration, and other manufactures deeply influenced people everywhere in the region, and many non-Anasazi communities had become virtually indistinguishable from those we call Anasazi.

During the tenth and eleventh centuries, when the size and number of Anasazi towns was increasing, similar growth was occurring in the south. Hohokam people expanded northward into mountainous and high valley country, where their irrigation techniques and architectural styles—so well suited to the hot southern deserts—were no longer practical. These northern Hohokam people adopted the successful methods of neighboring Mogollon and Anasazi groups. Many Mogollon communities in northeastern Arizona and central and southern New Mexico also experienced rapid growth. Their architectural and social solutions to the novel problems posed by larger community size seem to have been modelled on those developed by their nearest Anasazi neighbors.

The material remains of the many towns and villages built between the twelfth and fourteenth centuries in the Anasazi borderlands are so like variations on Anasazi themes that cultural classification becomes difficult, and the nature and extent of Anasazi expansion is problematical. For example, the early twelfth-century Wupatki ruin just north of the Mogollon Rim is a compact, multistory Sinagua culture town of over 100 rooms. It has Mesa Verde-like masonry, kivas, a Hohokam-style ball court, and Kayenta Anasazi-style pottery. Similar interactions had similar effects in the north where Fremont people were heavily influenced by their Kayenta Anasazi neighbors, and in the northern Rio Grande where other marginal agriculturalists were brought into the Chacoan Anasazi sphere.

Part of the Classic period Anasazi expansion was simply a function of population increase, part resulted from the accretion or recruitment of other peoples into Anasazi communities, and part was due to voluntary changes made in non-material and material aspects of their culture by communities and people who were not closely related to any of the Anasazi. In turn, these newly-made Anasazi no doubt changed the material and intellectual culture of the Four Corners and Rio Grande Anasazi, and succeeding generations of Anasazi and Pueblo people.

The material culture and intellectual lives of Mogollon people living in mountain valleys of southwestern New Mexico and southeastern Arizona were transformed by their adoption of Anasazi concepts and technologies. From the eleventh through the thirteenth centuries, community after community in that vast area moved from scattered pit house villages of only a few families each into above-ground pueblos that might have several hundred connected rooms built about a plaza or plazas. Their novel, kiva-like ceremonial chambers were rectangular, and some were as large as Chacoan Great Kivas. They built reservoirs fed by canals, terraced fields, check dams, and other public works. Some made black-and-white pottery that clearly derived from eastern Anasazi traditions; others took similar designs and applied them to Mogollon redwares. These adaptations generated many innovations that had important effects upon the Anasazi, then and later. Bold, curvilinear patterns that ultimately derived from the Hohokam were dynamically transformed by northern Mogollon and western Anasazi artists. New iconography was invented, which almost certainly came to the Anasazi incorporating new religious ideas that had profound effects. More certainly, these new motifs accompanied technological innovations in pottery making, including use of glaze paints and colored slips. The borderlands where cultures met became breeding grounds for invention and innovation.

In one way, the end of the Classic Anasazi period meant the end of all that. Whatever combination of internal and external impulses, environmental and intellectual forces that led the Anasazi to abandon their Four Corners homeland

82. Pottery bowl, Pinedale polychrome from the White Mountain area of east-central Arizona. The bold asymmetry and iconic forms suggest later Pueblo IV pottery designs while the strong negative patterns and linear precision are reminiscent of western Anasazi Pueblo III wares. Ht. 4 1/2". ca. 1300-1400. Laboratory of Anthropology, Museum of New Mexico, Santa Fe.

83. The Galaz site in the Mimbres Valley, ca. 1100. (Artist's reconstruction after LeBlanc: 1983.)

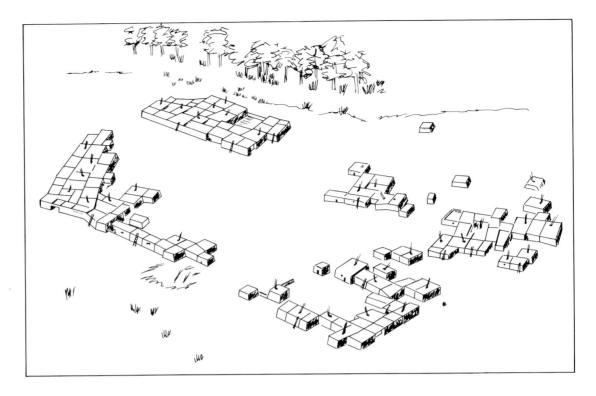

impacted just as severely on all other southwestern peoples. The Hohokam withdrew from the mountains and consolidated themselves in the low southern deserts of Arizona. The Mogollon moved out of their ancient mountain and desert homelands in southern New Mexico and southern Arizona, some as early as the twelfth century, but most in the thirteenth century. Fremont people withdrew to the northern deserts, abandoning their tentative grasp on a Kayenta Anasazi lifeway. The Sinagua, Salado and all of the others were all affected; all migrated to somewhere else. Many disappeared, simply lost to history as they merged with other groups. The Mogollon and Sinagua, whose material lives were so strongly affected by the Anasazi in the thirteenth century, merged with Anasazi people during the fourteenth century. Others did the same, and surely some Anasazi became Fremont or Hohokam people. The Pueblo IV Anasazi in their new land were a profoundly altered people.

Chapter Four

DISPERSION, RELOCATION, INVASION: A.D. 1300-1600

Overview: A.D. 1300-1600

The era beginning in about 1300, called "Pueblo IV" by the Pecos Conference in 1927, was also referred to by many culture historians earlier in our century[1] as the "Regressive Pueblo Period." It is a misleading name, for Pueblo IV was a time of creative change, growth, and innovation. There were more Anasazi people than ever before, and many more large towns than at any time in the past. This last Anasazi period bridges history and prehistory, ending in about 1598 with the first Hispanic settlements in New Mexico. Some authorities would date the Anasazi era end earlier, with the Coronado expedition of 1540, and some suggest that the end should date from the Hispanic reconquest following the Pueblo Revolt of 1680.

By 1300, the Anasazi had established new centers around the borders of their ancient homeland—east along the Rio Grande and upper Pecos River watersheds, south on the wooded plateaus above the Mogollon Rim, and west in the barren lands of the Hopi country. There was a vast reorganization of southwestern peoples, as groups formerly identified with Mogollon, Sinagua, Salado, and other cultures living along the frontiers of the Anasazi world were absorbed by these new towns. Anasazi people from the different Four Corners districts were also brought together in novel political and social configurations. New regional traditions evolved that, as in the past, are most sensitively defined by pottery styles.

Pottery styles were transformed by innovative, iconographic, aesthetic, and craft concepts, many of which were prefigured by late thirteenth-century inventions. Of particular importance were the polychrome and glaze-painting techniques that evolved, along with powerful new pictorial systems and iconography in the Anasazi-Mogollon border areas of western New Mexico and eastern Arizona, and in the southern Kayenta region. After the fourteenth century, polychrome wares, using new paint colors including black, green, and purple glazes on red, orange, or yellow slips, dominated the pottery of the Cibola and Rio Grande districts. Regional variations were pronounced. Rio Grande glaze wares are easily distinguished from those made in the Zuni-Cibola area; the Hopi in northeastern Arizona made unique use of yellow paste pottery; and carbon-paint designs on white or gray surfaces were now made only in some parts of the northern Rio Grande.

84. Pottery jar, carbon-painted Jemez black-on-white, Jemez Mountains district, New Mexico. Ht. 11″. Pueblo IV period, ca. fifteenth to seventeenth century. Indian Art Fund, School of American Research.

85.86. Two pottery bowls, Sikyatki polychrome, Hopi Pueblos. Pueblo IV period, fifteenth to seventeenth century. University Museum, University of Pennsylvania. Top: stylized bird, diameter 12 ¼″. Bottom: hand partially covering a flying bird, diameter 10 ¼″.

As in earlier times, pottery paintings were usually organized within panels that conformed to the architecture of a vessel, but that architecture had changed. Bowls were generally larger and more shallow and their rims tended to curve inward, suggesting a closed, jarlike shape. They were now painted on both visible surfaces. The dominant new jar form was a wide-mouthed, low vessel with a prominent neck and sloping shoulder, which became the focus for zoned design panels. Linearity was still important but hachuring was virtually abandoned, replaced by fields of color; and line quality was dramatically different—thicker, more fluid, at times almost sloppy. Figure-ground relationships were made more complex by the introduction of new colors and textures. Most painted vessels were probably made for secular purposes, but the old geometric elements and motifs were often recombined to become feathers, birds, sun symbols, kachina masks, and other sacred iconographic forms that give many painted vessels of this time a ritual character.

The Anasazi migrations took several centuries, having begun about the middle of the twelfth century, when many people left the Chaco Canyon area, continued until the Mesa Verde and Kayenta districts were abandoned by about 1300, and may still have been in progress at the time of first contact with Europeans. During those centuries, there were many smaller movements within the larger one. Some groups may have migrated several times from canyon to canyon within the Anasazi heartland, while others shifted more certainly toward its periphery. The process was gradual and piecemeal, and may not have been perceived at the time as radically different from the smaller-scale, periodic abandonments that had characterized the earlier history of most Anasazi people.

Coincident with the Anasazi movements to the south and east, more southerly peoples, especially subgroups of the Mogollon, moved northward, apparently with the same sort of steady but unfocussed inertia that moved the Anasazi. About the time that Chaco was abandoned, Mogollon people of the Mimbres Valley in southwestern New Mexico also moved, though we do not know where. They had earlier adopted Anasazi town planning and architectural concepts, and their black-on-white pottery was heavily influenced by Anasazi styles. To their east, Jornado Mogollon people built Anasazi-style villages during the 1200s and early 1300s as they moved northward, finally merging with eastern Anasazi groups during the fourteenth century. Further west, the high mountain valleys of the San Francisco and upper Gila River drainages supported hundreds of fair-sized Mogollon and Salado pueblos during the thirteenth century. All were abandoned by about 1400, their people joining with the Anasazi, and that great, fertile land became as empty of people as the San Juan Basin.

It is impossible today to identify any particular group of the Mogollon with any Anasazi or later Pueblo community, just as it is impossible to identify most older Anasazi ruins with any modern Pueblo. We can only be sure that, on the one hand, there was amalgamation of Mogollon and Anasazi people and, on the other, the Anasazi became Pueblo people.

During the fourteenth century, a number of novel ritual and cultural ideas seem to have been introduced to the Anasazi from Mexico, especially having to do with the supernaturals called *kachinas*. Pictures of kachinas, which were virtually unknown before then, appear in great number at rock art sites in and adjacent to Jornado Mogollon territory after about 1300. By 1350, kachina images dominated the rock art of the Anasazi, and became integral to the florescence of mural painting, which was a major art form of the Pueblo IV Period. Kachinas have much in common with supernaturals who are associated with water and fertility by many different peoples of northern Mexico. There is a profusion of those beings who may

87. Hopi shrine with clan symbols at Willow Springs near the Grand Canyon, Arizona.

be related to the Mesoamerican deity called Tlaloc, and they are thought to live in mountains, springs, or lakes. Southwestern rock art sites, with kachina images, are often found in the vicinity of those landscape features, and the kachinas themselves are thought to reside in mountains, lakes, or springs.

It is probable that the Anasazi thought of kachinas as benevolent beings whose blessings included rain, good crops, and fertility, but who were also dangerous and required prayers and ritual offerings of feathers, prayer sticks, and food. They were impersonated by use of masks, and their impersonators acted as intermediaries between ordinary humans and more distant deities. The personalities of the kachinas were assimilated with those of other supernaturals, including Cloud Spirits, and with ancestors and other human dead. Pueblo IV Kachina Societies were probably similar to those of the modern Pueblos. Membership would have been the minimum religious requirement for all men, and the Societies were integrated with other social and ceremonial institutions, including clans, moieties, kiva groups, and Medicine Societies. Their elaborate rituals were public and highly theatrical and, since only initiates could impersonate kachinas and thereby approach certain supernaturals, the Societies were essential for community welfare. The association of kachinas with ancestors may sometimes have been symbolized by clan signatures in the form of kachina masks and by other kachina images at places associated with the spirits of the dead.

How kachinas came to the Anasazi is a matter of debate. Casas Grandes had begun to decline during the thirteenth century and was overrun by about 1350, one of the few southwestern cases where there is evidence of a community destroyed by violence. Its violent end was symptomatic of unrest all along the northern frontier of Middle America, which may have been triggered by the political and military upheavals in the Valley of Mexico accompanying the fall of the Toltecs and culminating in Aztec dominance. The introduction of religious ideas to the Southwest may have been among the far-reaching effects of those distant events. While the sequence and mechanisms for those introductions are not clear, Jornado Mogollon rock art and Mimbres pottery painting may be evidence that transmission

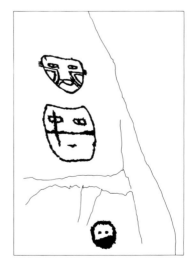

88. Pueblo IV petroglyphs of kachina masks at the site of Cerro de los Indios on the Rio Grande in central New Mexico. Largest mask about 18″ high. Fifteenth to seventeenth century.

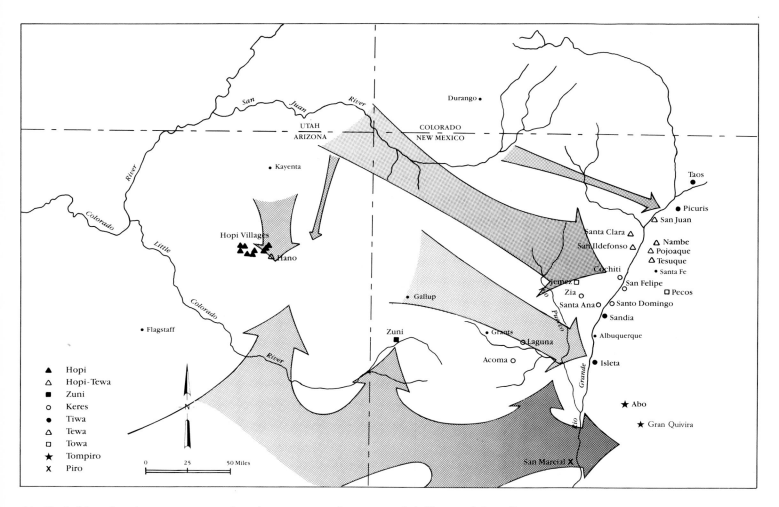

89. Probable migration routes leading to the Pueblo IV settlements at the time of the Spanish invasions. Pueblo languages are indicated.

to the Anasazi was by way of different Mogollon groups.

Warfare or fear of violence seems to have had an impact on the Mogollon even in their isolated and rugged mountain valleys. Many Mogollon villages of the twelfth to fourteenth centuries are walled and defensively situated, but more tangible evidence of violence is generally lacking both in Mogollon territory and in that of the far more vulnerable desert Hohokam. Among the Anasazi also, there is little evidence that violence and raiding were any more common than in earlier times. Nonetheless, many Pueblo IV towns have a decidedly defensive character, and there is ample evidence in sixteenth-century Hispanic documents that warfare was no stranger to the Anasazi.

The Southwest was considerably stabilized by the time of the first contacts with Europeans, and many Anasazi towns named in sixteenth-century Spanish records[2] were long established in their new locations, among them Pecos, Taos, and Acoma—all founded between about 1250 and 1400. Most of the towns that the Spanish called *pueblos* were located along the Rio Grande and its feeder streams in New Mexico between modern Taos in the north and San Marcial in the south. Many related communities[3] were east of the Rio Grande along the Pecos River and its tributaries, and there were clusters of towns near Acoma and Zuni in northwestern New Mexico and on, or near, the Hopi mesas of northeastern Arizona. The majority were at altitudes ranging from 4,500 to 6,600 feet in semiarid, temperate country, but with considerable differences in local environment. At Taos, for example, the growing season was short, but there were good permanent water sources and easy access to relatively rich and varied wild animal and vegetable foods. By contrast, at Acoma and Hopi, the growing season may have been a bit longer, but water was scarce and good hunting territories were less accessible.

Early Spanish chronicles describe the Anasazi as healthy, industrious, and moderately prosperous. Maize, beans, and squash were their staple cultivated foods, cotton was an important crop, and flocks of turkeys were kept at many places. Depending upon local conditions, a wide variety of water management techniques were practiced, including ditch irrigation and use of agricultural terraces. Game animals were the main source of animal protein and wild plants such as piñon nuts and amaranth were important for food as well as for their economic and medicinal value. The largest pueblos were multistoried, many-roomed, terraced houses built of stone or adobe. Blocks of rooms were usually arranged in a rectangular plan that enclosed a plaza within which were large circular or square kivas which the Spanish called *estufas*. Kivas and other ceremonial rooms were also placed within room blocks, sometimes in profusion.

Most towns were politically autonomous, and Spanish accounts note few obvious distinctions between the rich and poor or the powerful and humble inhabitants of these places. Governmental organizations were dominated by older men and a network of religious fraternal organizations. Inheritance of economic resources, including houses and agricultural rights, was often through the female line, and gender powers as well as gender roles were carefully balanced. Similarities to earlier

90. Taos Pueblo, model and photo by William Henry Jackson, 1877. Museum of New Mexico, Santa Fe.

189

91. Acoma Pueblo founded in the thirteenth century has a town plan that resembles the Pueblo III town of Yellow Jacket. Aerial view, ca. 1955. Museum of New Mexico, Santa Fe.

92. Petroglyph of a warrior, almost life-size, Comanche Gap, Galisteo Basin, north-central New Mexico. Pueblo IV, fifteenth to seventeenth century.

Anasazi political, religious, economic, and social institutions, technology, town planning, and styles in art are very great, while many of the differences can be attributed to changed environments. The influx of new peoples also had its effects, for example, by the introduction of new social and ritual institutions and of novel practises, such as that of cremation, amongst some Anasazi groups.

Easily worked sandstone, which had been fundamental to Anasazi architecture of the Four Corners, was a rarity in many parts of their new territory, as were natural rock shelters that could enclose cliff houses. Most of the larger towns were now built of sun-dried adobe walls laid in courses by the basket load and stabilized by the use of stone foundations and wooden stringers in the walls. They were usually located in open country near streams, or on mesa-top defensive sites. But, where stone suitable for masonry was available, it was used, and even where adobe replaced stone, the forms and aesthetic character of Pueblo IV communities closely resembled those of earlier times.

The defensive potential of the self-enclosed, large pueblos is obvious, and Spanish accounts of warfare with the Pueblos describe their defensive use. Spanish chronicles suggest that the Pueblo IV Anasazi had war societies, and pictures of warriors and their regalia in murals and rock art confirm that warfare was an important fact of life, integrated within their ritual system. But direct evidence of warfare is rare, and the earliest Spanish accounts also stress the peaceful and nonaggressive qualities of Pueblo IV society. Defense was a factor, but perhaps not the key one in the planning of these late Anasazi towns. As in earlier times, the closed spaces of inward-looking communities provided form and focus for tightly integrated, highly structured societies.

Tradition and the social role of architecture seem to have been critical factors in town planning, and the differences between Pueblo III and Pueblo IV solutions to community planning and construction problems may have more to do with materials than design. Calling Pueblo IV a "Regressive Period," because it is judged that there was a startling architectural decline, is really no more than distinguishing between the textures, colors, and degree of preservation of fine sandstone veneers and those of mud adobe walls. The differences may only reflect the fact that abandoned stone buildings can be beautiful long after adobe ones have melted back into the earth.

Ten or more separate Pueblo IV "provinces," and at least six different languages, were recognized by the Spanish. Political alliances and economic relationships cut across these linguistic barriers and overrode the cultural ones. The Pueblo IV Anasazi alternately fought and traded with their nonsedentary neighbors, sometimes fought with each other, and sometimes allied with non-Pueblo people against other Pueblo folk. Only once, in 1680, when they successfully revolted against Spanish domination is there a recorded instance of them acting in political concert. Even then, unity was never total, and it had shattered entirely by the time the Spanish returned to power in 1692.

The Rio Grande Anasazi: 1300-1600

There had been continuous Anasazi occupation of various parts of the Rio Grande drainage from Basket Maker times, but it was in many respects a marginal Anasazi territory until well into the 1200s. It was a region where people were as likely to live in small pit house villages as in pueblos, and to rely as much on hunting and gathering as on agriculture. In the southern parts of the area, Mogollon-like utilitarian brown-ware pottery might be made, and in the north, bag-shaped, brown or gray utility wares resembled pottery made by Plains Indian farmers living along western tributaries of the Mississippi and Missouri Rivers. Despite these provincial anomalies, these were Anasazi people. Their kivas—and presumably their ritual and social lives—were Anasazi, and their painted pottery, scarce as it was, was clearly Chacoan or Mesa Verde in style.

The Pueblo IV provinces of the Rio Grande described by the Spanish in the

93. Wall paintings inside a small cave at the Pueblo IV site of Cerro de los Indios, Rio Grande Valley, central New Mexico. Tallest figure about 4″. Note that the animal on the left wears a feathered headdress, has mountain lion claws and a rainbow back and tail. Fifteenth to sixteenth century.

sixteenth century were a vastly different and very complex group of communities. The most southern and eastern of them were prosperous towns that spoke several now extinct languages. Tompiro-speaking[4] people lived east of the Rio Grande in the Salinas Pueblos, so called because of their proximity to salt lakes that were the last remnants of Lake Estancia, a late Pleistocene sea. Their territory included high grasslands and wooded mesas, and they seem to have carried on an extensive trade in salt with many different groups. They were adjacent to the high plains and had contacts with Plains Indians, with whom they exchanged maize and salt for bison meat and dressed skins. Related Piro-speaking[5] people occupied mesas and terraces above the broad alluvial plains of the Rio Grande valley.

This had been Mogollon country until Anasazi towns were built in the fourteenth and fifteenth centuries, and the likelihood is that the Piro and Tompiro were, in fact, Mogollon people who became Anasazi. Their rock art was rich in kachina imagery and included some spectacular paintings in small rock shelters, as well as pecked and engraved pictures. Their pottery included polychrome glaze and matte-painted wares related to both the dominant Rio Grande Pueblo IV tradition and that of Zuni to the west. Their practise of cremation, as well as inhumation, also suggests Zuni relationships. And yet, because they lived in one of the few places in eastern Anasazi country where suitable stone was available, their masonry buildings, even the Hispanic mission churches, are superficially similar to those of the Classic period Anasazi.

North of the Salinas Pueblos, in the Estancia and Galisteo Basins, were other large masonry and adobe towns occupied by Tano speakers[6] and at least one, Pecos Pueblo, where Towa was spoken.[7] There may have been as many as 3,000 residents of Pecos in the sixteenth century, and it was a notable trading center in contact directly or indirectly with the Pacific coast, central Mexico, and the Mississippi valley. The inhabitants made beautiful stone axes for trade, and maize, skins, meat, pottery, and many other goods were regularly exchanged with both Anasazi and alien peoples. Some of the Tano towns were almost as large as Pecos, but they seem primarily to have been residences for agricultural people who preferred to live in large and defensible places. The local rock art suggests very active War and Kachina Societies.

The area had been heavily settled late in the thirteenth century by people whose carbon-painted pottery was derived from Mesa Verde. The Tano speakers may have been among the first emigrants from Mesa Verde, while the Towa, whose nearest linguistic relatives lived some sixty miles to the east, probably migrated from northwestern New Mexico. By late in the fourteenth century, both groups were making polychrome glazeware pottery in the Rio Grande-style that is barely distinguishable from that made by most other eastern Pueblo IV Anasazi people. If not for the written accounts of sixteenth-century Spanish observers, there would be little reason to suspect that the different towns were occupied by ethnically and linguistically distinct peoples.

North of the Piro settlements, in the vicinity of modern Albuquerque, were Tiwa-speaking[8] people living in a large number of adobe towns located on the Rio Grande flood plain and on terraces just above it. Some that had more than a thousand rooms and were several stories high are now low, barely visible earthen mounds, and others have disappeared, washed away by periodic floodwaters of the Rio Grande or destroyed by modern urban growth. Two southern Tiwa towns still exist, and the inhabitants of the most northerly of the Rio Grande Pueblos—Taos and Picuris—which are located in high, heavily wooded mountain valleys, also speak Tiwa. Taos has been continuously occupied since the fourteenth century and is the last remaining large adobe town with terraced buildings that still convey the

94. Petroglyphs near Pueblo Blanco, Galisteo Basin, north-central New Mexico. Pueblo IV, fifteenth to seventeenth century. Tallest figure about 22".

107. *Pueblo IV rock engraving from Cerro de los Indios, middle Rio Grande Valley, bordering former Jornado Mogollon territory. The figure has iconographic similarities to Smoking Mirror, Mexican Lord of the Night and opposite of Quetzalcoatl. Ht. 3'. Fifteenth century.*

108. *Pueblo* IV *ornaments of shell, turquoise, and Arizona pipestone. Longest pendant is 2 ¹/₂". Laboratory of Anthropology, Museum of New Mexico, Santa Fe.*

109. *Pottery jar, Bandelier black-on-gray, Pajarito Plateau, northern Rio Grande. Wide-mouthed, squat jars and large, low bowls with incurved rims characterize pottery shapes of the Pueblo* IV *era in most districts. Ht. 9¹/₂". ca. 1400-1550. Indian Art Fund, School of American Research, Santa Fe.*

110. *Two Pueblo IV glaze polychrome pottery bowls. Left: Rio Grande glaze* C *vessel, Santa Fe area, New Mexico, ca. 1450-1500; right: Hawikuh polychrome, mid seventeenth century, Zuni region. Ht. 6". Novel shapes and colors, use of exterior designs, and iconic imagery such as feathers and dragon flies are characteristics of Pueblo IV domestic and ritual pottery. Indian Art Fund, School of American Research, Santa Fe.*

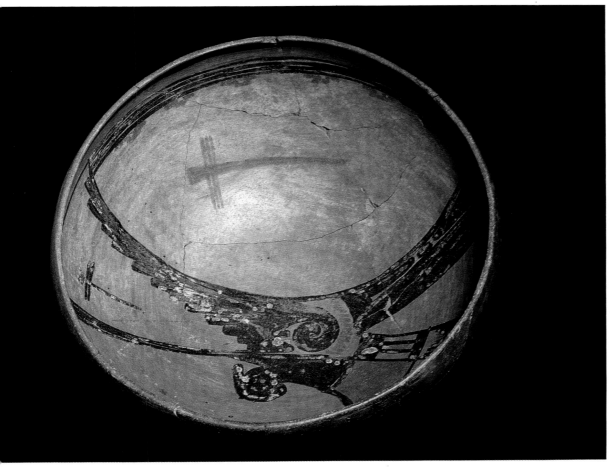

111. *Pottery bowl, Pottery Mound glaze polychrome, middle Rio Grande Valley. The yellow slip, bold asymmetries, and iconic character all resemble Sikyatki-style wares from Hopi, several hundred miles away. Kiva murals at the Pottery Mound site also resemble contemporaneous Hopi kiva art. Ht. 4". ca. 1440-1490. Maxwell Museum of Anthropology, Albuquerque.*

112. Painted kiva at the
Pueblo IV site of Kuaua, Rio
Grande Valley, New Mexico.
(Replica.) The original
paintings probably date from
ca. 1450-1500.

Opposite:

113. Engraved rock picture
of a masked hunter and a
large crane at the Pueblo IV
Piro site of Cerro de los
Indios, New Mexico. Crane
is 40" high.

Following pages:

114. Painted kachina images
in a shallow rock shelter near
the Salinas Pueblo of
Tenebo, New Mexico.
Ht. of shelter, 6'.

115. Late Pueblo III and early Pueblo IV carbon-painted pottery of the Rio Grande district. The two bowls are Wijo black-on-white, ca. 1325-1400; the canteen is Santa Fe black-on-white, ca. 1225-1350. The canteen is 6 ¹/₂" high. Laboratory of Anthropology, Museum of New Mexico, Santa Fe.

Following pages:

116. Selenite pendants, Rio Grande Pueblo IV Anasazi. Longest is 5". Laboratory of Anthropology, Museum of New Mexico, Santa Fe.

117. The large sixteenth-century site of Tyonyi in Frijoles Canyon, Pajarito Plateau, New Mexico. Looking toward the Rio Grande.

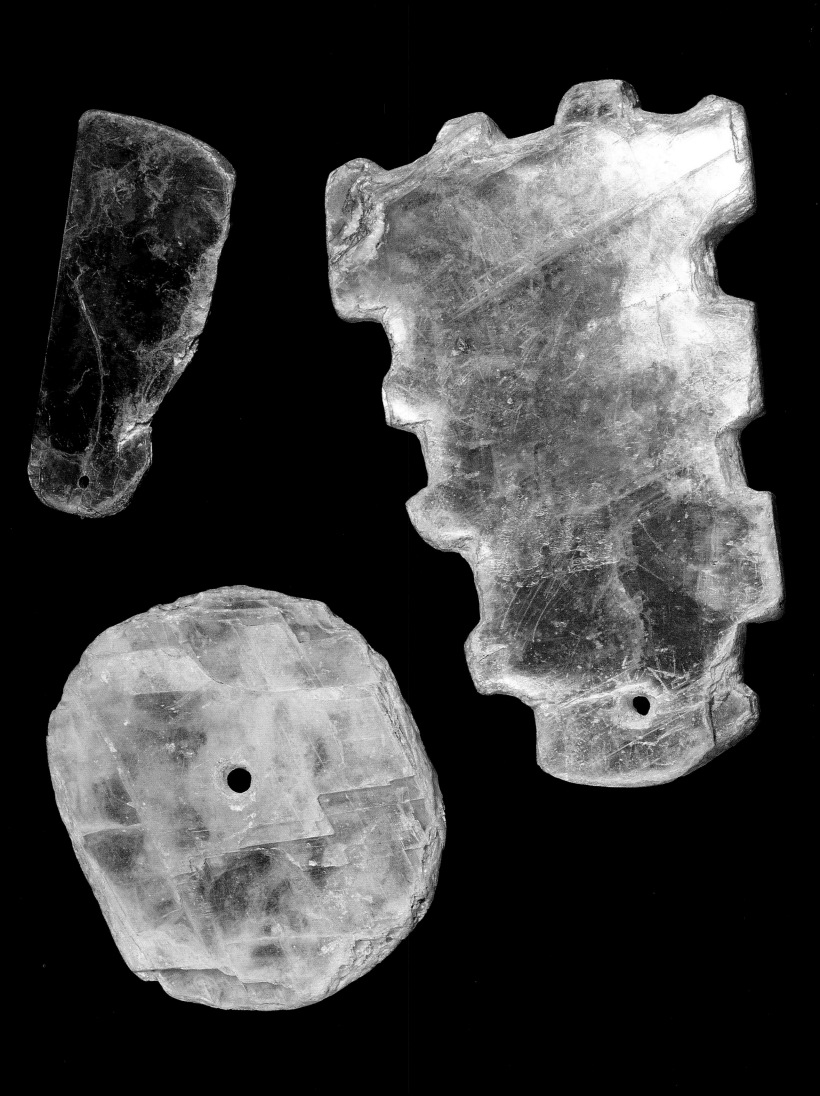

118. 119. *Pueblo IV site of
Tsankawi on the Pajarito
Plateau, New Mexico. The
niches carved in the soft
volcanic ash are doorways to
rooms that were never
completed. Late
sixteenth century.*

120. Ruins of the Spanish
mission at Gran Quivira,
New Mexico, largest of the
Salinas Pueblos, abandoned
ca. 1670.

Following pages:

121. The fifteenth- and
sixteenth-century Pueblo IV
site of Sapawe in the Chama
River Valley, adjacent to the
Pajarito Plateau, northern
Rio Grande district, New
Mexico. The six plazas clearly
seen here were enclosed by
multi-storied building blocks
totaling more than 1000
residential rooms.

122. The Stone Lion shrine
on the Pajarito Plateau, New
Mexico, is at least as old as
the Pueblo IV period and is
still used by Pueblo people
who come from as far away
as Zuni to make
offerings here.

character of the Pueblo IV communities.

Both the northern and southern Tiwa still live about where their ancestors had lived for the last thousand years. They seem to be descended from the original Rio Grande Anasazi people and were probably linked by other Tiwa-speaking villages until about 1300, when new peoples entered the middle Rio Grande Valley. By the fourteenth century, Kachina Societies were strong among the southern Tiwa, as evidenced by rock art and rare kiva murals uncovered at several towns that predate the European intrusions. This valley was also an important production area of Rio Grande glaze polychrome pottery which, along with textiles, was strongly influenced after about 1400 by Hopi decorative ideas. The northern Tiwa apparently never shared in the rich ceremonialism of the Kachina Societies, and they rarely (if ever) made painted pottery. Taos, however, was an important trading center, serving as middleman between the more southerly, agriculturally productive Rio Grande Anasazi and the nomadic, hunting tribes of the Rocky Mountains, the Plains, and the eastern San Juan Basin.

North and west of the Tiwa and intermingled among them were many Keresan-speaking[9] communities and the Towa-speaking Jemez towns. Jemez and some Keresan pueblos were on the southern edge of the high, heavily forested, volcanic Jemez Mountains, with their great outcrops of obsidian and basalt, and on the deeply layered volcanic ash that forms the mesas and deep canyons of the Pajarito Plateau on its eastern side. Other Keresan towns were on the southern part of the Pajarito Plateau and at Acoma, almost 120 miles to the southwest.

Five of the modern Keresan Pueblos can be traced to sites of the Pueblo IV era and some even to Pueblo III ancestral homes. All have traditions[10] that tell of several stages in their migration to the Rio Grande and, while a Chacoan origin seems likely, they mingled with other peoples during their travels and now trace their beginnings to Mesa Verde as well as Chaco. Some traveled with Jemez people, who were a provincial, northern New Mexico Anasazi group heavily influenced by Mesa Verdean styles in architecture and pottery from Pueblo I through Pueblo III times. Others lived alongside Tewa-speaking people in the Chama Valley and on the Pajarito Plateau during the Pueblo IV period, and their pottery and architecture came to resemble that of the Tewa. All Pueblo IV Keresan towns had Kachina Societies, as evidenced by their art and documented in sixteenth-century Spanish chronicles.[11]

The Tewas also participated in the Kachina Society system. They appear to have moved out of the Mesa Verde region at the end of the Classic Pueblo period and, over the next 200 years, built a sequence of large adobe towns that are now reduced to low mounds of earthen rubble along the Chama River, a tributary of the Rio Grande in northwestern New Mexico. Some had as many as 1,000 rooms, carefully laid out in a gridwork that enclosed large, open plazas containing several big, round kivas. By 1500, they had built stone and adobe pueblos of similar form on the Pajarito Plateau and along the Rio Grande between the Keresans and the northern Tiwa. And, in many places where the Pajarito Plateau is cut by canyons, they excavated cavelike dwellings out of the soft volcanic ash that became the inner rooms and kivas of multistoried pueblos. They farmed the river valleys, narrow canyon bottomlands, and mesa tops, building appropriate water and soil management devices as needed.

Some of the Pajaritan cave structures superficially resemble Classic Period cliff houses of the Mesa Verde and Kayenta regions. The ground plans of their enclosed surface pueblos range from circular to rectangular, and are consistent with Pueblo III town planning everywhere. Their large, circular kivas are similar to Chaco Great Kivas. Tewa pottery resembles other Pueblo IV Rio Grande ceramics in form and patterning but is a carbon-painted gray or cream-colored ware with a peculiar, soft and gritty paste called "biscuit ware," made by mixing Pajaritan clay with volcanic ash. This was almost the only eastern Anasazi pottery that was not a glaze polychrome. It is derived from Mesa Verde traditions, heavily modified by the glaze polychrome styles of the western Anasazi and southern Rio Grande. As is the case throughout the Anasazi world in the Pueblo IV era, the Tewa incorporated and reinterpreted ideas, concepts, and institutions from many parts of the Southwest and made them their own.

The Western Anasazi, Zuni-Cibola: A.D. 1300-1600

The Coronado Expedition came to Zuni in 1540 in search of the wealth of the legendary seven cities of Cibola. There were then about 6,000 Zuni people living in six towns rather than seven cities, and they had no gold, but the Spanish nevertheless identified them and their land with fabled Cibola. This Zuni-Cibola-Little Colorado region was the borderland in western New Mexico and eastern Arizona between the Anasazi and the Mogollon, and included the Keresan town of Acoma. It is mesa and mountain country, forested and well watered, but with short growing seasons because of the high elevation. Much of it is on the Pacific Ocean side of the Continental Divide, drained by the Zuni and Little Colorado Rivers which flow northward to join the Colorado River east of the Grand Canyon.

There was an apparent population increase throughout the Zuni-Cibola district in the thirteenth century caused, at least in part, by movement of Mogollon people northward and Anasazi people southward. A number of large towns in Classic Pueblo style were built in the area of blocky masonry. Many of them, including Acoma and Atsinna, which lies about midway between Acoma and Zuni, are sited defensively on high mesas.

Keresan Acoma was built in about 1250 in a spectacular location on a high, steep-walled sandstone mesa in arid country very like that of Chaco Canyon. Anasazi people had lived near Acoma from Basket Maker times; several Chaco outliers,

95. Acoma Pueblo. Photo by Ben Wittick, ca. 1885-90. Museum of New Mexico, Santa Fe.

abandoned not long before Acoma was built, are nearby and, until the fourteenth century, local pottery was in the Chacoan tradition. While Acoma ancestors most likely included Chaco people, the town's masonry is crude compared to that of Classic era Chaco, its kivas are square like those of the western Anasazi and neighboring Mogollon, its open town plan is similar to Yellow Jacket at Mesa Verde, and its Pueblo IV glaze paint pottery is more like that of Zuni than of the Rio Grande Keresans. In all these respects, Acoma illustrates both the complexity of Pueblo IV history and the fact that language alone is a poor diagnostic of Anasazi ethnic identity.

Atsinna is among the places considered directly ancestral to Zuni. It had about 1,000 rooms, Anasazi-style round kivas and Mogollon square ones, and dates from the thirteenth to the late fourteenth centuries. It is one of many places in the eastern Zuni-Cibola area that were abandoned in about 1400, at about the time that the Zuni towns first visited by the Spanish, such as Halona and Hawikuh, were established. Anasazi people had lived in the Zuni area from Basket Maker times, and several large Chaco outliers were built there, most notably the Village of the Great Kivas which was occupied from about 1100 to 1200. It was after then that the vigorous fusion of Chacoan Anasazi and mountain Mogollon people and communities began in this region. Use of both round and square kivas and glaze polychrome pottery may be the most visible evidence of that melding, but it is witnessed in many other ways. For example, some Pueblo IV Zuni people buried their dead following Anasazi procedures while others practised cremation, a custom that was almost certainly derived from the Hohokam, though it may have come to Zuni by way of some Mogollon or Salado group. And, it is likely also that mortuary offerings of "killed" pottery—vessels with holes punched in them at the time of burial—came directly or indirectly to Zuni from Mimbres Mogollon people.

The Zuni language is unrelated to any other Pueblo IV tongue and, in fact, to any

96. Zuni Pueblo, Halona, from the Zuni River. Waffle gardens are similar to the eleventh-century fields excavated at Chetro Ketl. Photo by Jesse L. Nusbaum, 1912. Museum of New Mexico, Santa Fe.

other known language. It may be a creole language, originally invented so that the peoples of a polyglot community could communicate with each other.[12] If so, it is a case where a *lingua franca* ultimately replaced all the original languages of a heterogeneous society. The origin legends of the different clans and ritual societies of Zuni also support an assumption of heterogeneity and fusion, with many indications of Mogollon, Salado, and even Hohokam origins for different groups that came to the Zuni-Cibola country after about 1250. There are indications that such diversity is even older for, despite the ceramic and architectural evidence of a strong Chaco presence in Pueblo III times, the basic Zuni origin myth has them emerging from the Grand Canyon, well within the Kayenta district.

About forty miles west of Zuni is the sacred lake that is the home of their dead, their unborn, their kachinas and other deities. Other Zuni religious shrines are located throughout the Southwest, some as far as 200 miles away. Clearly, Zuni was formed by diverse peoples, but, regardless of origins, by late Pueblo IV times the Zuni were a cohesive group living along a twenty-five-mile stretch of the wide Zuni River valley. There, they irrigated their farmlands and hunted deer and other game in nearby highlands. Their towns were built of blocky stone, two or three stories high or higher, terraced, and each had several plazas where outdoor rituals were held. Their kivas were square or rectangular, and at least some of them were contained within the room blocks. Each town was governed independently, but they shared elaborate ritual and social systems as well as language and would band together for defense, taking refuge when necessary on top of the high and sacred mesa known as Dowa Yolanne, "Corn Mountain" in English.

Zuni was the Center Place of the Zuni people, but it was also located near the center of the Pueblo IV Anasazi world. Trading parties came there from all over the Southwest, and it seems to have acted as a redistribution center in a widespread trading network. Zuni controlled access to a large salt lake, wove textiles, cured buckskin and other animal hides, and likely had surplus meat and maize to exchange for feathers and bird skins, turquoise, shell, and other exotic goods. Their glaze polychrome pottery was very widely traded and had great influence upon the evolution of Pueblo IV pottery styles among all of the eastern Anasazi. It is also likely that then, as now, their control of sacred knowledge attracted the interest of other Anasazi and alien people. Trading parties from Pecos Pueblo, more than 180 miles to the east, visited there regularly, and Zuni men seem also to have travelled great distances on trading expeditions. It appears that Zuni[13] may have filled some of the roles that had once been played by the Chaco towns.

The Western Anasazi, Hopi: A.D. *1300-1600*

The lush landscapes of Zuni-Cibola, the Jemez Mountains, and the northern Tiwa regions of the Rio Grande Valley are in sharp contrast to the dessicated Hopi country. The Hopi mesas are located along the south end of Black Mesa, which extends northward for 120 miles and encompasses about a third of the territory of the Kayenta Anasazi. At the time of first contact with the Spanish in 1540, there were seven terraced Hopi towns, larger than those of Zuni, and they all spoke Hopi,[14] which is a Shoshonean language related to those of the Great Basin northwest of the Colorado Plateau. It is conceivable that this was the dominant language of the Kayenta Anasazi who settled in the Hopi country in about 1300. Their towns were located atop high, steep-walled mesas, and in some cases the town plan was dictated by the size and shape of the limited space available. Room blocks generally surrounded small, rectangular plazas, and there was a profusion of

rectangular kivas, some in room blocks, others in plazas. Construction was of crude, blocky stone masonry.

Betatakin at the north end of Black Mesa was the ancestral home of one Hopi clan, others trace their origins to Kayenta people of Canyon de Chelly, and still others to those from Tusayan in the Grand Canyon area. But not all Hopi migrated at the end of the Pueblo III era, for some were in their country already. The Hopi mesas had been occupied by Kayenta people from Basket Maker times, and at least one modern town, Oraibi, dates from the thirteenth century. Other of the large sixteenth-century towns were as old as Oraibi, and many Pueblo IV Hopi people were surely descended from those very ancient Anasazi residents.

There are many Hopi clans and ritual societies, and, as at Zuni, their traditions and origin legends have them coming from all directions to their present homes. Hopi kachinas live in a lake high on the San Francisco Peaks, visible on the western horizon about ninety miles distant. Other sacred shrines are in the Grand Canyon to the northwest, and in various locations southward and eastward. Ancestral towns are identified among Sinagua ruins along the Mogollon Rim and in the Verde Valley, and Hohokam, Salado, and Mogollon origins for some Pueblo IV Hopi also seems likely. There are legendary relationships as well with virtually all of the eastern Pueblo peoples, some of which date back to the Pueblo IV era. However, by the sixteenth century, there was considerable unity amongst all the Hopi, albeit with somewhat more obvious diversity than was the case at Zuni.

There are no permanent streams or rivers in Hopi country, and in Pueblo IV times the Hopi people were absolutely dependent upon local rainfall and water from springs and shallow wells, usually located at the base of the mesas upon which they lived. The aridity of the country is dramatized by a landscape that has virtually no top soil and is punctuated by sand dunes. Yet their livelihood depended upon agricultural products: maize, beans, squash, and cotton supplemented by game

97. The Hopi Pueblo of Oraibi. Photo by Frederick H. Maude, 1896. Museum of New Mexico, Santa Fe.

98. Peach trees, beans, corn, and chilies grow in the sand dunes near the modern Hopi pueblos in northeastern Arizona. Similar farming practices using sand as mulch to conserve scarce water were invented by the Anasazi ancestors of modern Pueblo people.

animals and wild foods such as piñon nuts. Their agricultural techniques not only involved all possible mechanical means for conserving and diverting water, but also included exploiting the unusual properties of their barren land. Because the sand dunes soaked up water rather than allowing it to run off, they protected aquifers that were four to six meters below the surface. Over generations, ancient Hopi farmers, through careful selection, developed maize and bean plants that germinated at depths of fifteen to twenty inches and sent deep roots down to the aquifers. This seed stock allowed use of the sand dunes as surprisingly efficient and high-yielding agricultural fields.

Perhaps not so surprisingly, an intense concern for water and fertility and the ethics of conservation and cooperation seems to have permeated all aspects of Pueblo IV Hopi life. If the visible and tangible remains of that era accurately reflect the realities of the time, then religion and ritual, especially as expressed through the Kachina Societies, permeated all secular activities and public and private institutions. Kachina imagery dominates the rock art of the period, especially that found at distant locations that are now religious shrines and the focus of pilgrimages. It is also expressed in a very rich mural painting tradition and in secular as well as religious pottery painting. Without doubt, the most intense and varied expressions of any Anasazi Kachina Societies occurred at Hopi, beginning in the early fourteenth century and continuing to the present day. And at Hopi, perhaps more than anywhere else, the kachinas monitored the behavior of the people, instructing, rewarding, and punishing adults as well as children to establish the norms and values of a well-mannered, useful, and proper way of life.

Hundreds of kiva murals, dating from the fourteenth through the seventeenth centuries, have been recovered from two Pueblo IV Hopi towns on Antelope Mesa, Awatovi and Kawaika-a. Other paintings of the same era, which are closely related to these Hopi traditions, have been recovered from several Rio Grande pueblo sites. Among them are hundreds of woven, dyed, and painted textiles, costumes, body paintings, masks, painted objects on wood and leather, pictures made with feathers, and other ephemeral art forms that would otherwise be entirely lost to us. These not only provide some sense of the beauty and elaboration that the Pueblo IV people created and invested in their rituals, but they also give insights to the spiritual and intellectual life of these Anasazi people. Many of the depicted objects are directly related to things used in the ritual and secular lives of modern Pueblo people.

For example, some murals show constructions that resemble altars used in modern Pueblo rituals of Kachina and Medicine Societies, and others represent activities, masks, costumes, and background scenery similar to those used today in theatrical performances of a religious and instructive nature. The decorative iconography in most murals is dominated by cloud forms, sunflowers, rosettes, and other images still used by modern Pueblos as emblems of rain and fruition. Many of these also appear on pottery paintings and other secular arts of the Pueblo IV era but, at Hopi more than elsewhere, the fusion of secular utility and religious iconography seems to be most obvious. It would appear that paintings of all sorts were made to inspire and instruct the Anasazi people as well as to decorate their everyday furnishings.

The Pueblo IV Hopi made unslipped, yellow pottery of highly polished, hard-firing clay. These distinctive wares were traded everywhere, and imitated in some places, especially the middle Rio Grande Valley, where orange or yellow slips were sometimes used on red or gray paste pottery. The black, mineral-based paint used by the Hopi fired to a brownish color with a shiny, glazelike texture. Red and white slips were also used as paint, usually to fill in delineated areas with blocks of color. A unique variety of textures including spatter, dry brush, incising, and engraving enlivens the picture surfaces. Designs include abstracted birds, feathers, sun symbols, and rain and cloud symbols, as well as realistically drawn birds, humans, other animals, and masks. Some pottery paintings are narratives, and others are very like complex images found in kiva murals both at Hopi and in Rio Grande towns.

Both representational and decorative pottery paintings are generally organized in spirals around the center of a vessel; most are symmetrical, but a large minority are unusually asymmetrical. They are usually framed with heavy lines that may be left open. This deliberate line break appears to be the first use of a visual metaphor seen in later Rio Grande pottery paintings and still used in some modern Pueblo art to ensure a flow of harmony between a picture and the outside world.

Hopi painted pottery of the Pueblo IV era exerted many strong influences upon all Rio Grande pottery painting styles. The combination of painterly qualities, iconography, and metaphor in secular Pueblo IV Anasazi pottery paintings is related to contemporary ritual art traditions as seen in kiva murals. As in earlier times, pottery painting was on a continuum with other kinds of pictorial art but, in the Pueblo IV period, its position appeared to shift from the domestic and mundane toward the esoteric and the sacred. The iconography and art of the Pueblo IV

99. Serigraph copy by Louie Ewing of a fifteenth- or sixteenth-century kiva mural from the Hopi town of Awatovi. (After Smith: 1952.)

215

Anasazi seem to have expressed an overt and affective spirituality that was quite different from anything known in the Anasazi past.

Anasazi Neighbors and the Spanish Entradas: A.D. 1300-1600

When the Spanish came to the Southwest 250 years after the Four Corners had been abandoned, the former Anasazi heartland was populated by small, scattered bands of people including Utes, Navajos, and Apaches, who were unrelated to either the Anasazi or any later Pueblo group. Some may have come into the area as early as the thirteenth century and conceivably had a role in forcing some Anasazi from their ancient homes. But there is little evidence to support such a premise and, while some traditional histories are explicit about warfare between some of these bands and Pueblo people after about the seventeenth century, they are silent on the matter before then. In fact, Navajo origin legends explicitly describe the ancient Anasazi lands as empty and the towns abandoned at the time the Navajo first arrived.

In any event, during the Pueblo IV era, relationships between the Anasazi and any of these latecomers seem to have varied considerably. They were all nomadic, hunter-gatherer peoples when they came into the region but some, especially groups of Navajo who had taken up residence along the San Juan River and in eastern Kayenta areas, had adopted Anasazi agricultural practises and rituals before the beginning of the sixteenth century. Their settlement patterns were not dissimilar to those of Basket Maker people, and their subsistence system, which balanced agriculture with hunting and gathering, is also reminiscent of marginal Anasazi people of earlier times. Those Navajo people and some Pueblo IV Anasazi certainly exchanged economic and ritual information and perhaps even intermarried. But relationships with other of the nonsedentary peoples were probably limited to occasional trade of maize for meat, other wild foods, and dressed animal skins. Some amount of raiding and other kinds of warfare certainly took place also. But it is unlikely that raiding by any of the nomadic groups represented more than an occasional annoyance before the introduction of the horse following Coronado's 1540 exploration.

During the remainder of the sixteenth century, until Juan de Oñate's 1598 expedition, there were several minor incursions by Spanish exploratory parties. Few of the early contacts with the Pueblo IV Anasazi were peaceful. Coronado had come to Zuni along a corridor just west of the Arizona-New Mexico border and soon made contact with all Anasazi districts. There were skirmishes and battles at Zuni, Hopi, and Acoma, which quickly destroyed any goodwill that might have developed between the Europeans and western Anasazi people. The Coronado party wintered among the southern Tiwa and fought even more bitterly with them and other eastern Anasazi. Later Spanish parties travelled up the Rio Grande or Pecos River valleys with similar bellicose consequences.

By Oñate's time, a pattern of animosity between the Spanish and most Anasazi peoples was well established. Many of the southern Rio Grande Anasazi towns were abandoned between 1540 and 1598, perhaps as a consequence of illnesses introduced by the Europeans, perhaps out of a desire to avoid violence. In any case, by the end of the sixteenth century the Spanish were not welcome among any of the southern Anasazi and established their first colony where prior contacts had been limited, among the northern Tewa, just east of the Pajarito Plateau. By 1610, they were well established and the Anasazi era had ended.

Chapter Five
AFTERWARDS: THE ANASAZI HERITAGE

Most sixteenth-century Spanish expeditions to the Southwest brought Mexican Indians with them who were sometimes able to communicate with Anasazi people in the Nahuatl language. The dominant language of the Valley of Mexico, Nahuatl was also used by many northern Mexican peoples (although not by any Anasazi group) and it was the *lingua franca* of ancient Mexican traders. Some Mexican Indians remained among the Anasazi, and some Anasazi were taken to Mexico by the Spaniards. The ancient ties with the south that had evidently continued during late Anasazi times were now modified and strengthened during the Hispanic era, for the seat of Spanish power was in far distant Mexico City.

From the Hispanic perspective, the Anasazi presented a moral and ethical responsibility, for they were a civilized group of souls in need of salvation by conversion to Spanish Catholicism. In addition, their land had geopolitical importance as a buffer zone to insulate the wealthy Middle American Spanish colonies from rival French and British New World interests. Beyond those issues, Anasazi country seemed to have limited economic value and was likely to be a drain on Spanish resources. Two generations passed between the initial explorations and colonization and, even then, the first Spanish colonies were small, impoverished villages and ranches, isolated from Spanish Mexico by poor roads, great distances, and hostile tribes.

Most Hispanic settlers were farmers, largely left to their own resources and intent on carving out a new life in a new land. They were potential competitors with the Anasazi pueblos for the same resources, but the land was vast and the peoples segregated, both by the Catholic Church represented by the Franciscan Order and by local Spanish government. The number of Spanish settlers was never large, and their physical presence was generally limited to the Rio Grande drainage. Nonetheless, within a short time, their impact was felt throughout the Pueblo world. Institutions had to be devised by the Pueblos to deal with the alien legal, political, military, and economic presence. New foods were introduced, including grains, vegetables, fruit, and domestic animals, that improved the Pueblo diet and lessened dependence on hunting. Horses were among the new animals and, when these became available to surrounding non-Pueblo people, raiding and warfare became serious problems. The Pueblos were also exposed to new diseases. The first smallpox epidemic struck in about 1640 and, within a century, smallpox and other European diseases played a significant role in reducing their population to about 10,000 and the number of their towns to about twenty. And, from the beginning, the Spanish made vigorous efforts to suppress native religions and convert the Anasazi to Catholicism.[1]

In other material respects, the European impact was almost minimal. Metalworking and carpentry with metal tools were about the only novel craft techniques brought to the Southwest by the first Spanish settlers. There were, in fact, so few craftsmen among them that they depended upon the Pueblos for necessities such as pottery containers and textiles. The influence on Anasazi material culture from the relatively few Franciscan missionaries who, during the first decades of the seventeenth century, established missions at many Anasazi pueblos, was only slightly greater. The ruins of their structures that remain today are massive stone buildings which dominate the native settlements. They were built by Pueblo labor with local materials according to plans supplied by the missionaries but, except for the introduction of metal tools, their technological impact was slight. Their architecture was visually and formally compatible with existing Pueblo stylistic traditions, and they merged nicely with the domestic buildings of the pueblos that they dominated.

With the exception of a few portable artifacts, including most of the essential tools of their trade which they brought with them, the Franciscans also depended upon Pueblo craftsmen. Religious pictures may have been done by the relatively unskilled priests, but the more decorative paintings in the churches, even those with European motifs, were generally painted by Indian women directed by the missionaries. Despite all novelties of form and function, most seventeenth-century Catholic ritual artifacts used in the pueblos were either made by Pueblo artists or were relatively crude products made by unskilled European priests.

Resentment of efforts to suppress native religions led to many violent episodes and generally unsuccessful proselytization. Several of the massive missions, such as

100. Pottery bowl, Zuni Pueblo, Ashiwi polychrome. Following the Spanish reconquest, glazeware vessels were no longer made but the bold patterns and iconography of the Pueblo IV period continued. Ht. 6". ca. 1730. Indian Art Fund, School of American Research.

101. Wall painting on the east wall of the Franciscan mission church at the Jemez Pueblo of Guisewa, ca. 1625. Photographer unknown. Museum of New Mexico, Santa Fe.

Guisewa near Jemez Pueblo, that were built during the 1620s, were abandoned within a few years, and others were destroyed by the Pueblos both before and during the Pueblo Revolt of 1680. Even where missionaries were most successful, as among the Salinas Pueblos, their success was superficial, and events conspired to defeat them. Destructive raids by the Apaches, economically ruinous demands of Spanish mission and civil authorities, and smallpox combined, by 1672, to force the Salinas people to abandon both their older villages and their newly built missions. More northerly Pecos Pueblo, once the largest of all, began a long decline at about the same time for similar reasons, also despite a moderately successful mission program.

The religious repressions, the dreadful epidemics, the raids by newly aggressive Apache, Navajo, Ute, and Plains tribes led to the successful Pueblo Revolt of 1680, which drove the Spanish out of the Southwest until the Reconquest of 1692. Hispanic rule was more relaxed after that, and the Church more tolerant, ultimately withdrawing from aggressive missionary work. Surviving Pueblos developed several methods for coping with disruptive religious influences. The eastern Pueblos, surrounded by Hispanics, synthesized some forms of Catholicism with their ancient Anasazi religions and practised many rituals in secret, most especially those having to do with the Kachina Societies. The western Pueblos, almost out of reach of Spanish political and military power, were more independent. Ancient Awatovi was destroyed by other Hopis when it welcomed the return of Catholic missionaries in 1700; almost 200 years passed before another Christian mission was established at Hopi. Zuni was also overtly hostile, and both places still openly practise their ancient rituals. Meanwhile, the Spanish residents were also distressed by diseases and the raiding of the nonsedentary tribes. The two groups of village and town dwellers had much in common and learned to coexist and to develop mutual support systems, especially as the military and economic power of Spain declined and its most distant North American province was forced to fend for itself.

When Mexican independence came about in 1821, the Pueblo population, although much reduced, still amounted to about twenty-five percent of the total population in all of New Mexico, including what is now the state of Arizona. The proportion of Pueblo people living within the boundaries of Pueblo IV Anasazi territory was very much higher. Occupation by the Americans a quarter century later had little immediate demographic impact but, by 1880, the incoming railroads signaled the beginning of the massive influx of new people that continues to the present day. The year 1880 then marks the beginning of a new set of radical changes in relationships between the Pueblo people and all other groups. It is only since then that the Pueblo descendants of the Anasazi people have been a demographically, as well as a politically, overwhelmed minority in their own land.

These Pueblo-Anasazi people do more than survive. They remain on their own land, surrounded by the sacred mountains and shrines that define their ancient heritage and their position within this physical universe. They are a diversity of peoples still, only nineteen pueblos now, but each incorporating within its singularity separate towns, villages, clans, ritual societies, curing societies, fraternities, and sororities. They are devoted to nurturing, balancing, and harmonizing these diversities, for each has its place and all would be diminished if one were lost. They are a microcosm of our complex and potentially chaotic universe. Their rituals and philosophies, ethics and world-view are all directed toward preserving, sustaining, and harmonizing nature and culture, past, present, and future. The traditional Pueblos are still the Anasazi.

Notes to the Text

PREFACE

1. See Kubler (1962).

CHAPTER 1

1. Sixteenth-century Anasazi people spoke at least the following languages which are still in use except where noted: 1) Hopi, a Shoshonean (Numic) language of the Uto-Aztecan family; 2) Tiwa, Tewa, Towa, Tano, and the now extinct Piro, Tompiro, and Humanas languages of the Kiowa-Tanoan family; 3) at least seven dialects of Keresan which seems to be a unique language family; and 4) Zuni, whose linguistic affiliations are also not known. See Hale and Harris (1979).
2. See Ortiz (1979) for detailed discussions of Southwestern archaeology and of Pueblo history and ethnology.
3. See Cordell (1984:49-119) and Willey and Sabloff (1980) for fuller discussions of the intellectual background of Southwestern archaeology.
4. Place names such as Aztec, Montezuma Castle, and Montezuma Valley, given by late nineteenth-century Anglo-Americans to archaeological sites and other locations in many parts of the Southwest demonstrate how popular was the notion of a link between the ancient Southwest and high cultures of Mexico. An early rail line still operating in New Mexico and Colorado was even named the "Cumbres and Toltec Railroad." Scholarly interest in prehistoric Mexican-Southwestern contacts continues. See DiPeso (1968), Holien (1974), Kelley and Kelley (1974), Riley and Hedrick (1978), and Schaafsma and Schaafsma (1974) among many others.
5. The meeting at Zuni between Coronado and a trading party from Pecos Pueblo is described in the narratives of the Coronado Expedition. See Hammond and Rey (1940).
6. See Riley (1971; 1975; 1978) for discussions of trade, language, and other communications between the prehistoric Southwest and Mesoamerica. Eckholm (1942) discusses contacts between western Mexico and the Southwest that informed the Spanish about Pueblo IV Anasazi in the early sixteenth century.
7. The fullest description of Hohokam culture is in Haury (1976).
8. Cordell (1984:107-113) argues for a later beginning of Pioneer period Hohokam than given by Haury (1976).
9. The term "Pueblo" derives from the Spanish word for "town," and originally only distinguished between aboriginal town-dwellers and more nomadic peoples. In the Southwest the term evolved to become almost synonymous with the word "tribe." In some cases (for example modern Hopi) a Pueblo may include a dozen or more towns; in others (for example Picuris) it refers to only a single community. Just as the number of communities that make up a single Pueblo may vary, so also the total number of Pueblos is variable. Laguna Pueblo did not exist until the seventeenth century and, in the twentieth century, at least two (Pojoaque and Nambe) that

were considered to be extinct or on the verge of extinction have been revived. It is unwise to conceive of the Pueblos as anything but dynamic.
10. See Bolton (1930) and Hammond and Rey (1940) for histories of the Coronado expedition as told by its several chroniclers.

CHAPTER 2

1. See Ferguson and Hart (1985) for maps and descriptions of the multi-faceted Zuni world, and Ortiz (1972b) for a description and analysis of Tewa cosmology. Ortiz (1979), Parsons (1939), Stephens (1936), and many ethnographic monographs offer other insights to the world-view of the various Pueblos.
2. The 1927 Pecos Conference was organized by A. V. Kidder and held at Pecos Pueblo where he was excavating. Virtually all archaeologists then active in the Southwest attended, including Frank H. H. Roberts, Neil Judd, Jesse Nusbaum, Earl Morris, Emil Haury, and Byron Cummings. Questions of nomenclature as well as classification and chronology were addressed. The Conference has since been revived and is held periodically at different Southwestern locations.
3. Ferguson and Rohn (1987) assign the very early date (700 B.C.) for Basket Maker II. Cordell (1979, 1984), Plog (1979), and Stuart and Gauthier (1981) are among many who would have the era begin no earlier than about A. D. 1.
4. Virtually all published chronological syntheses including Ferguson and Rohn (1987) as well as the others cited in Note 3 above are in agreement about the transition dates from Basket Maker II to Basket Maker III.
5. Because the Pecos Classification is intended to be a developmental scheme rather than a chronological one, Frank H. H. Roberts (1935) suggested that it be modified to reduce its chronological implications. In Roberts' system the sequence goes: Basket Maker; Modified Basket Maker; Developmental Pueblo; Great Pueblo; Regressive Pueblo; Historic Pueblo.

CHAPTER 3

1. A remarkable number of well-planned, complex research programs have been conducted in many parts of the Southwest in recent decades. Among the more notable are intensive studies of the Chaco System in the 1970s and 1980s at the Chaco Center, a joint project of the National Park Service and the University of New Mexico directed by Robert L. Lister and then by W. James Judge. The National Park Service, University of Colorado, and other institutions and agencies began comprehensive studies at Mesa Verde and in the Montezuma Valley in the 1960s. Some still continue. Lister, Arthur B. Rohn, Joe Ben Wheat, Alden Hayes, David

Breternitz, and Bruce Bradley are among many investigators involved. Elsewhere, a massive research program was conducted at Black Mesa, Arizona, directed by George Gummerman of Southern Illinois University. Space precludes citing equally important investigations conducted by the University of Arizona, University of Utah, and other institutions.

2. A brief, comprehensive discussion of recent studies at Chaco Canyon is given in Lekson, Windes, Stein, and Judge (1988).

3. Sherd temper analyses conducted by the Chaco Center support the view that large quantities of pottery were brought to Chaco Canyon from the Chuska Mountains to the west. See Toll (1984).

4. Average annual rainfall at Chaco Canyon is about 8 inches (Williams 1986:45).

5. See Ferguson and Rhone (1987) for a more elaborate discussion of the Far View Community.

6. In general, small kivas range in size from about 12 to 20 feet in diameter (or to a side if square or rectangular), and Great Kivas from about 45 to 70 feet. Intermediate sized kivas are also known.

7. See Lange, Mahaney, Wheat, and Chenault (1986), and Ferguson and Rhone (1987:123-135) for discussions of Yellow Jacket Ruin and the Montezuma Valley. Sand Canyon Pueblo is currently being excavated under direction of Bruce Bradley for the Crow Canyon Research Center.

8. Cryptic emblems such as small animals and triangular motifs that are occasionally found on the bottoms of mugs and bowls, and variations in rim tick patterns suggest identification marks of workshops or even of individual potters.

9. See Ellis (1967), Ford, Schroeder and Peckham (1972), and Schroeder (1979) for discussions of archaeological, linguistic, and ethnographic evidences of Pueblo III—Pueblo IV migrations.

10. The late Charles DiPeso of the Amerind Foundation directed research at Casas Grandes for many years. Volumes 1-3 of the massive reports of that work (DiPeso et. al., 1974) provide a stimulating synthesis.

CHAPTER 4

1. See Kidder (1927) and Roberts (1935).

2. See Schroeder (1979) for a concordance (including maps) of the many identifiable pueblos mentioned by sixteenth-century Spanish chroniclers including those with the Coronado expedition (1540), the Rodrigues-Chamuscado party (1581-1582), Espejo (1582-1583), Castaño de Sosa (1590), and Oñate (1598). See Simmons (1979) for a summary history of Indian-Spanish realtionships in the Southwest.

3. The summary descriptions given here of the sixteenth-century Anasazi is of linguistically related communities that were generally (but not always) in geographical proximity to each other. The political, social, ritual, ethnic, and economic relationships between many of these towns before they were classified by the Spanish as "provinces" on the basis of language affiliation is not always clear and may have been quite variable.

4-9. See Note 1, Chapter 1 for information about linguistic relationships of the Pueblo languages.

10. Keresan origin legends are recorded by Stevenson (1894), White (1932; 1935; 1942; 1962), and Stirling (1942). See also the Keresan Pueblos described in Ortiz (1979).

11. Images of kachinas are commonplace in Pueblo IV and historic era kiva murals and rock art in all areas except (possibly) Taos and Picuris. Coronado in 1540 alluded to water-related Anasazi ritual art, but the earliest written descriptions of Anasazi ritual paintings and carvings that were probably of kachinas was by members of the Rodriguez-Chamuscado expedition in 1581-82, only the second intrusion into the Southwest. In 1598, Villagra (who was with the Oñate colonizing expedition) was explicit in describing kachina-like deities that he saw painted on a kiva wall at a Tiwa town. There are many mentions of kachina masks after colonization, and by the mid-seventeenth century they were routinely being destroyed by Spanish missionaries (Dutton 1963:3-18; Kessell 1980; Schroeder 1979:237; Smith 1952).

12. See Ford, Schroeder, and Peckham (1972) and Hale and Harris (1979) for overviews of Pueblo prehistory that discuss possible Anasazi linguistic affiliations.

13. There is a wealth of publications concerning Zuni from Cushing (1896), and Stevenson (1904), through Bunzel (1932 a and b), to Tedlock (1972;1979), Ladd (1983), and Ferguson and Hart (1985).

14. Except for the Hopi-Tewa people who migrated to the Hopi First Mesa early in the eighteenth century and still speak Tano (southern Tewa), a Kiowan-Tanoan language, the Hopi people speak Hopi, a Shoshonean (Numic) language of the Uto-Aztecan family.

CHAPTER 5

1. See Kessell (1979; 1980), Schroeder (1979), and Simmons (1979) for detailed discussions of the impact upon the Anasazi of the Hispanic invasions of the American Southwest.

Bibliography

AMBLER, RICHARD J.
1977   *The Anasazi*, (Flagstaff: Museum of Northern Arizona).

ANDERSON, FRANK G.
1955   "The Pueblo Kachina Cult: A Historical Reconstruction," *Southwestern Journal of Anthropology*, vol. 11, no. 4:404-419, (Albuquerque).

BANDELIER, ADOLF F.
1890-1892   "Final Report of Investigations Among the Indians of the Southwestern United States, Carried on Mainly in the Years from 1880 to 1885," *Archaeological Institute of America, Papers, American Series*, vol. 3 (Part I), vol. 4 (Part II), (Cambridge, Mass.).

BEAGLEHOLE, ERNEST
1936   "Hopi Hunting and Hunting Ritual," *Yale University Publications in Anthropology*, no. 4, (New Haven).

BENEDICT, RUTH R.
1931   "Tales of the Cochiti Indians," *Bureau of American Ethnology Bulletin* 98, (Washington, D.C.: Smithsonian Institution).

BERRY, MICHAEL S.
1982   *Time Space and Transition in Anasazi Prehistory*, (Salt Lake City: University of Utah Press).

BINFORD, LEWIS R.
1971   "Mortuary Practices: Their Study and Their Potential," in "Approaches to the Social Dimensions in Mortuary Practices," ed. James A. Brown, *Society of American Archaeology, Memoir* 25: 6-29.

BLISS, WESLEY L.
1936   "Problems of the Kuaua Mural Paintings," *El Palacio*, vol. 40, nos. 16, 17, 18:81-87, (Santa Fe).

BOLTON, HERBERT E.
1930   *Spanish Exploration in the Southwest 1542 - 1706*, (New York: Charles Scribner's Sons).

BOURKE, JOHN G.
1884   *The Snake Dance of the Hopi*, (New York: Charles Scribner's Sons).

BRAND, DONALD D.
1938   "Aboriginal Trade Routes for Sea Shells in the Southwest," *Yearbook, Association of Pacific Coast Geographers*, vol. 4:3-10.

BRAND, DONALD D., F. M. HAWLEY, F. C. HIBBEN, AND D. SENTER
1937   "Tseh So, a Small House Ruin, Chaco Canyon, New Mexico, Preliminary Report," *University of New Mexico Bulletin, Anthropological Series*, vol. 2, no. 2, (Albuquerque).

BRETERNITZ, DAVID A.
1966   "An Appraisal of Tree-Ring Dated Pottery in the Southwest," *Anthropological Papers of the University of Arizona*, 10, (Tucson).

BREW, JOHN O.
1940   "Mexican Influence Upon the Indian Cultures of the Southwestern United States in the 16th and 17th Centuries," in *The Maya and Their Neighbors*: 341-348, ed. C. L. Hay et al., (New York: D. Appleton-Century).
1944   "On the Pueblo IV and on the Kachina-Tlaloc Relations," in "El Norte de Mexico y Sur de Estados Unidos," Tercera Reunion de Mesa Redonda Sobre Problemas Antropologicos de Mexico y Centroamerica: 241-245, *Sociedad Mexicana de Antropologia*, no. 3, (Mexico City: Castillo de Chapultepec).
1946   "Archaeology of Alkali Ridge, Southeastern Utah," *Peabody Museum, Harvard University, Papers*, vol. 21, (Cambridge).

BRILL, LOIS SONKISS
1984   *Kokopelli: An Analysis of his Alleged Attributes and Suggestions Toward Alternate Identifications*, M. A. Thesis, (Albuquerque: University of New Mexico).

BRODY, JERRY J.
1969-1972   "The Kiva Murals of Pottery Mound," in *Proceedings of the 38th International Congress of Americanists*, vol. 2:101-110, (Stuttgart-Munich).
1977   *Mimbres Painted Pottery*, (Albuquerque: School of American Research and University of New Mexico Press).
1984   "Chacoan Art and the Chaco Phenomenon," in *New Light on Chaco Canyon*: 13-18, ed. David Grant Noble, (Santa Fe: School of American Research).
1989   "Site Use, Pictorial Space, and Subject Matter in Late Prehistoric and Early Historic Rio Grande Pueblo Art," *Journal of Anthropological Research*, vol. 45, no. 1:15-28, (Albuquerque: University of New Mexico).

BROWN, JAMES A.
1971   "Approaches to the Social Dimensions in Mortuary Practices," *Society of American Archaeology, Memoir* 25.

BULLARD, WILLIAM R., JR.
1962   "The Cerro Colorado Site and Pithouse Architecture in the Southwestern United States Prior to A.D. 900," *Papers of the Peabody Museum of American Archaeology and Ethnology*, 44(2), (Cambridge: Harvard University).

BUNZEL, RUTH
1932a   "Zuni Kachinas," *Bureau of American Ethnology, 47th Annual Report*: 837-1086, (Washington, D. C.: Smithsonian Institution).
1932b   "Introduction to Zuni Ceremonialism," *Bureau of American Ethnology, 47th Annual Report*: 467-544, (Washington, D. C.: Smithsonian Institution).

CAPERTON, THOMAS J.
1981   "An Archaeological Reconnaissance of the Gran Quivira Area," in *Contributions to Gran Quivira Archaeology, Publications in Archaeology* 17:3-11, ed. Alden C. Hayes, (Washington D. C.: National Park Service).

CARLSON, ROY L.
1970   "White Mountain Redware: A Pottery Tradition of Eastcentral Arizona and Western New Mexico," *Anthropological Papers of the University of Arizona* 19, (Tucson).

COHODAS, MARVIN
1978   "Style and Symbolism in the Awatovi Kiva Mural Paintings," *Phoebus* 1:9-21, (Phoenix and Tucson).

COLTON, HAROLD S.
1960   *Black Sand: Prehistory of Northern Arizona*, (Albuquerque: University of New Mexico Press).

CORDELL, LINDA S.
1979   "Prehistory: Eastern Anasazi," in *Handbook of North American Indians*, vol. 9, Southwest: 131-151, ed. Alfonso Ortiz, (Washington, D. C.: Smithsonian Institution).

1984   *Prehistory of the Southwest*, (Orlando: Academic Press, A School of American Research Book).

CORDELL, LINDA S., AND FRED PLOG
1979   "Escaping the Confines of Normative Thought: A Reevaluation of Puebloan Prehistory," *American Antiquity*, vol. 44, no. 3:405-429.

COSGROVE, CORNELIUS B.
1947   "Caves of the Upper Gila and Hueco Areas in New Mexico and Texas," *Peabody Museum, Harvard University, Papers*, vol. 24, no. 2, (Cambridge).

COURLANDER, HAROLD
1982   *Hopi Voices,* (Albuquerque: University of New Mexico Press).

CROTTY, HELEN K.
1983   "Honoring the Dead: Anasazi Ceramics from the Rainbow Bridge - Monument Valley Expedition," *Museum of Cultural History, UCLA, Monograph Series*, no. 22, (Los Angeles).

CUSHING, FRANK HAMILTON
1883   "Zuni Fetiches," *Bureau of American Ethnology, Second Annual Report*:9-45, (Washington, D. C.: Smithsonian Institution).

1896   "Zuni Creation Myths," *Bureau of American Ethnology, Thirteenth Annual Report*:321-447, (Washington, D. C.: Smithsonian Institution).

DeHARPORT, DAVID L.
1951   "An Archaeological Survey of Canyon de Chelly: Preliminary Report of the Field Sessions of 1948, 1949, and 1950," *El Palacio*, vol. 58, no. 2:35-48, (Santa Fe).

DiPESO, CHARLES C.
1968   "Casas Grandes and the Gran Chichimeca," *El Palacio*, vol. 74, no. 4: 45-61, (Santa Fe).

1979   "Prehistory: Southern Periphery," in *Handbook of North American Indians*, vol. 9, Southwest:152-161, ed. Alfonso Ortiz, (Washington, D.C.: Smithsonian Institution).

DiPESO, CHARLES C., JOHN B. RINALDO, AND GLORIA J. FENNER
1974   *Casas Grandes: A Fallen Trading Center of the Gran Chichimeca*, vols. 1 - 3, (Dragoon, Arizona: Amerind Foundation).

DITTERT, ALFRED E., JR. AND FRED PLOG
1980   *Generations in Clay: Pueblo Pottery of the American Southwest*, (Flagstaff: Northland Press).

DOCKSTADER, FREDERICK J.
1954   *The Kachina and the White Man*, (Bloomfield Hills, Mich.: Cranbrook Academy of Science).

DOZIER, EDWARD P.
1954   "The Hopi-Tewa of Arizona," *University of California Publications in American Archaeology and Ethnology* 44(3):259-376, (Berkeley).

1970   *The Pueblo Indians of North America*, (New York: Holt, Rinehart and Winston).

DUTTON, BERTHA P.
1963   *Sun Father's Way*, (Albuquerque: University of New Mexico Press).

1964   "Mesoamerican Culture Traits which Appear in the American Southwest," *Actas, 35th International Congress of Americanists*:481-492, (Mexico City).

1983   *American Indians of the Southwest*, (Albuquerque: University of New Mexico Press).

ECKHOLM, GORDON F.
1942   "Excavations at Guasave, Sinaloa, Mexico," *American Museum of Natural History, Anthropological Papers*, no. 38:23-139, (New York).

ELLIS, FLORENCE HAWLEY
1967   "Where Did the Pueblo People Come From?", *El Palacio*, vol. 74:35-43, (Santa Fe).

FERGUSON, T. J., AND E. RICHARD HART
1985   *A Zuni Atlas*, (Norman: University of Oklahoma Press).

FERGUSON, WILLIAM M., AND ARTHUR H. ROHN
1987   *Anasazi Ruins of the Southwest in Color*, (Albuquerque: University of New Mexico Press).

FEWKES, J. WALTER
1903   "Hopi Kachinas as Drawn by Native Artists," *Bureau of American Ethnology,* 21st Annual Report for the Years 1899-1900:13-126, (Washington, D. C.: Smithsonian Institution).

1904   "Two Summers' Work in Pueblo Ruins," *Bureau of American Ethnology,* 22nd Annual Report for the Years 1900-1901, Part 1:1-196, (Washington, D. C.: Smithsonian Institution).

1909   "Antiquities of the Mesa Verde National Park: Spruce Tree House," *Bureau of American Ethnology, Bulletin* 41, (Washington, D. C.: Smithsonian Institution).

1911   "Antiquities of the Mesa Verde National Park: Cliff Palace," *Bureau of American Ethnology, Bulletin* 51, (Washington, D. C.: Smithsonian Institution).

1919   "Designs on Prehistoric Hopi Pottery," *Bureau of American Ethnology,* 33rd Annual Report for the Years 1911-1912:207-284, (Washington, D. C.: Smithsonian Institution).

FORD, RICHARD I.
1972   "An Ecological Perspective on the Eastern Pueblos," in *New Perspectives on the Pueblos*:1-18, ed. Alfonso Ortiz, (Albuquerque: University of New Mexico Press).

FORD, RICHARD I., ALBERT H. SCHROEDER, AND STEWART L. PECKHAM
1972   "Three Perspectives on Puebloan Prehistory," in *New Perspectives on the Pueblos*:19-39, ed. Alfonso Ortiz, (Albuquerque: University of New Mexico Press).

FRISBIE, THEODORE R. (ED.)
1974   "Collected Papers in Honor of Florence Hawley Ellis," *Papers of the Archaeological Society of New Mexico*, no. 2, (Norman: Hooper Publishing Co.).

FRISBIE, CHARLOTTE (ED.)
1980   *Southwestern Indian Ritual Drama*, (Albuquerque: University of New Mexico Press).

GLADWIN, HAROLD S.
1957   *A History of the Ancient Southwest*, (Portland, Maine: The Bond Wheelwright Co.).

GLADWIN, HAROLD S., EMIL W. HAURY, EDWIN B. SAYLES, AND NORA GLADWIN
1938   "Excavations at Snaketown I: Material Culture," *Medallion Papers* 25, (Globe, Arizona: Gila Pueblo).

GUERNSEY, SAMUEL J., AND A. V. KIDDER
1921   "Basketmaker Caves of Northeastern Arizona," *Papers of the Peabody Museum of American Archaeology and Ethnology* 8(2), (Cambridge: Harvard University).

GUNNERSON, JAMES H.
1969   "The Fremont Culture: A Study in Cultural Dynamics on the Northern Arizona Frontier," *Peabody Museum, Harvard University, Papers*, vol. 59, no. 2, (Cambridge).

HALE, KENNETH, AND DAVID HARRIS
1979   "Historical Linguistics and Archaeology," in *Handbook of North American Indians*, vol. 9, Southwest:170-177, ed. Alfonso Ortiz, (Washington, D. C.: Smithsonian Institution).

HAMMOND, GEORGE P., AND AGAPITO REY
1940   *Narratives of the Coronado Expedition 1540-1542*, (Albuquerque: University of New Mexico Press).

1966   *The Rediscovery of New Mexico 1580-1594: The Explorations of Chamuscado, Espejo, Castano de Sosa, Morlete, and Leyva de Bonilla and Humana*, (Albuquerque: University of New Mexico Press).

HAURY, EMIL W.
1936   "The Mogollon Culture of Southwestern New Mexico," *Medallion Papers* 20, (Globe, Arizona: Gila Pueblo).

1945 "The Problem of Contacts Between the Southwestern United States and Mexico," *Southwestern Journal of Anthropology*, vol. 1:54-74, (Albuquerque: University of New Mexico).

1950 *The Stratigraphy and Archaeology of Ventana Cave*, (Tucson: University of Arizona Press).

1976 *The Hohokam: Desert Farmers and Craftsmen*, (Tucson: University of Arizona Press).

HAWLEY, FLORENCE

1950 "Big Kivas, Little Kivas, and Moiety Houses in Historical Reconstruction," *Southwestern Journal of Anthropology*, vol. 6, no. 3:286-302, (Albuquerque: University of New Mexico).

HAYES, ALDEN C., (ED.)

1981a *Excavation of Mound 7, Publications in Archaeology 16*, (Washington, D. C.: National Park Service).

1981b *Contributions to Gran Quivira Archaeology, Publications in Archaeology 17*, (Washington, D. C.: National Park Service).

HAYES, ALDEN C., D. BRUGGE, AND W. J. JUDGE

1981 *Archaeological Surveys of Chaco Canyon, New Mexico, National Park Service Publications in Archaeology 18A*, (Washington, D. C.:National Park Service).

HEDRICK, BASIL C., J. CHARLES KELLEY, AND CARROLL L. RILEY (EDS.)

1974 *The Mesoamerican Southwest*, (Carbondale: Southern Illinois University Press).

HEWETT, EDGAR L.

1938 *Pajarito Plateau and its Ancient People*, (Albuquerque: University of New Mexico Press).

HIBBEN, FRANK C.

1975 *Kiva Art of the Anasazi at Pottery Mound*, (Las Vegas, Nevada: K. C. Publications).

HILL, JAMES N.

1970 "Broken K Pueblo: Prehistoric Social Organization in the American Southwest," *Anthropological Papers of the University of Arizona 18*, (Tucson).

HODGE, FREDERICK W.

1937 "History of Hawikuh, One of the So-Called Cities of Cibola," *Publications of F. W. Hodge Anniversary Fund*, vol. 1, (Los Angeles: Southwest Museum).

HOLIEN, THOMAS

1974 "Pseudo-Cloisonné in the Southwest and Mesoamerica," in "Collected Papers in Honor of Florence Hawley Ellis," ed. Theodore Frisbie, *Papers of the Archaeological Society of New Mexico*, no. 2.

IRWIN-WILLIAMS, CYNTHIA

1973 *The Oshara Tradition: Origins of Anasazi Culture*, Eastern New Mexico University Contributions in Anthropology, vol. 5, (Portales).

1979 "Post-Pleistocene Archaeology, 7000-2000 B.C," in *Handbook of North American Indians*, vol. 9 Southwest:31-42, ed. Alfonso Ortiz, (Washington, D. C.: Smithsonian Institution).

JENNINGS, JESSE D.

1966 "Glen Canyon: A Summary," *Anthropological Papers of the University of Utah 81*. Glen Canyon Series 31, (Salt Lake City).

1978a *Ancient Native Americans*, (San Francisco: W. H. Freeman).

1978b "Prehistory of Utah and the Eastern Great Basin," *Anthropological Papers of the University of Utah 98*, (Salt Lake City)

JENNINGS, JESSE D., AND E. NORBECK (EDS.)

1964 *Prehistoric Man in the New World*, (Chicago: University of Chicago Press).

JENNINGS, JESSE D., AND ERIK REED

1956 "The American Southwest: A Problem in Cultural Isolation," *Society for American Archaeology, Memoir 11*.

JERNIGAN, WESLEY E.

1978 *Jewelry of the Prehistoric Southwest*, (Albuquerque: University of New Mexico Press).

JUDD, NEIL M.

1930 "The Excavation and Repair of Betatakin," *United States National Museum, Proceedings*, vol. 77, art. 5, Publications no. 2828, (Washington, D. C.)

1954 "The Material Culture of Pueblo Bonito," *Smithsonian Miscellaneous Collections*, vol. 124, (Washington, D. C.)

1964 *The Architecture of Pueblo Bonito*, Smithsonian Miscellaneous Collections 124, (Washington, D. C.).

JUDGE, W. JAMES

1984 "New Light on Chaco Canyon," in *New Light on Chaco Canyon*, ed. David Grant Noble, (Santa Fe: School of American Research).

JUDGE, W. JAMES, W. B. GILLESPIE, STEPHEN H. LEKSON, AND H. W. TOLL

1981 "Tenth-Century Developments in Chaco Canyon," *Archaeological Society of New Mexico Anthropological Papers 6*, (Santa Fe).

JUDGE, W. JAMES, AND JOHN D. SCHELBERG

1984 "Recent Research on Chaco Prehistory," *Reports of the Chaco Center*, no. 8, Division of Cultural Research, National Park Service, (Albuquerque).

KELLEY, J. CHARLES

1966 "Mesoamerica and the Southwestern United States," in *Handbook of Middle American Indians*, vol. 4, ed. Robert Wauchope, (Austin: University of Texas Press).

1974 "Speculations on the Culture History of Northwestern Mesoamerica," in *The Archaeology of West Mexico*, ed. Betty Bell, (Ajijic, Jalisco: West Mexican Society for Advanced Study).

KELLEY, J. CHARLES, AND ELLEN ABBOTT KELLEY

1974 "An Alternative Hypothesis for the Explanation of Anasazi Culture History," in "Collected Papers in Honor of Florence Hawley Ellis," *Papers of the Archaeological Society of New Mexico*, no. 2, ed. Theodore Frisbie.

KENT, KATE PECK

1945 "A Comparison of Prehistoric and Modern Pueblo Weaving," *The Kiva*, vol. 10, no. 2:14-20, (Tucson: University of Arizona).

1983 *Prehistoric Textiles of the Southwest*, (Albuquerque: University of New Mexico Press).

KESSELL, JOHN L.

1979 *Kiva, Cross, and Crown: the Pecos Indians of New Mexico 1540-1840*, (Washington D. C.: National Park Service, U. S. Department of the Interior).

1980 *The Missions of New Mexico*, (Albuquerque: University of New Mexico Press).

KIDDER, ALFRED V.

1927 "Southwestern Archaeological Conference," *Science*, vol. 66: 489-491.

1932 "The Artifacts of Pecos," *Papers of the Southwestern Expedition*, no. 6, (New Haven: Phillips Academy).

1962 *An Introduction to the Study of Southwestern Archaeology with a Preliminary Account of Excavations at Pecos* [1924], (New Haven and London: Yale University Press).

KIDDER, ALFRED V., AND SAMUEL J. GUERNSEY

1919 "Archaeological Explorations in Northeastern Arizona," *Bureau of American Ethnology, Bulletin 65*, (Washington, D. C.: Smithsonian Institution).

KIDDER, ALFRED V., AND ANNA O. SHEPARD

1936 "The Pottery of Pecos [vol. 2]. The Glaze Paint, Culinary, and Other Wares," *Papers of the Southwest Expedition 7*, (New Haven: Phillips Academy and Yale University Press).

KUBLER, GEORGE

1962 *The Shape of Time*, (New Haven: Yale University Press).

1972 *The Religious Architecture of New Mexico in the Colonial Period and Since the American Occupation*, (Albuquerque: University of New Mexico Press).

LADD, EDMUND

1983 "Zuni Religion and Philosophy," *Exploration, Zuni*

El Morro: Past and Present:26-31, ed. David G. Noble, (Santa Fe: School of American Research).

LAMBERT, MARJORIE F.
1954   "Pa-ako, Archaeological Chronicle of an Indian Village in North Central New Mexico," *School of American Research Monograph* no. 19, (Santa Fe).

LAMBERT, MARJORIE F., AND J. R. AMBLER
1961   "A Survey and Excavation of Caves in Hidalgo County, New Mexico," *School of American Research Monograph*, no. 25, (Santa Fe).

LANGE, CHARLES H., AND CARROLL L. RILEY (EDS.)
1966   *The Southwestern Journals of Adolph F. Bandelier*, (Albuquerque: University of New Mexico Press).

LANGE, FREDERICK, NANCY MAHANEY, JOE BEN WHEAT, AND MARK L. CHENAULT
1986   *Yellow Jacket: A Four Corners Anasazi Ceremonial Center*, (Boulder: Johnson Books).

LEBLANC, STEVEN A.
1983   *The Mimbres People: Ancient Pueblo Potters of the American Southwest*, (London: Thames and Hudson).

LEHMER, D. J.
1948   "The Jornado Branch of the Mogollon," *Social Science Bulletin* 17, University of Arizona Bulletin 19(2), (Tucson).

LEKSON, STEPHEN H. (ED.)
1983   "The Architecture and Dendrochronology of Chetro Ketl, Chaco Canyon, New Mexico," *Reports of the Chaco Center*, no. 6, (Albuquerque: Division of Cultural Research, National Park Service).

1986   *Great Pueblo Architecture of Chaco Canyon, New Mexico*, (Albuquerque: University of New Mexico Press).

LEKSON, STEPHEN H., THOMAS C. WINDES, JOHN R. STEIN, AND W. JAMES JUDGE
1988   "The Chaco Canyon Community," *Scientific American*, vol. 259, no. 1:100-109.

LINDSAY, ALEXANDER J., AND JEFFERY S. DEAN
1981   "The Kayenta Anasazi at A.D. 1250: Prelude to a Migration," *Proceedings of the Anasazi Symposium*, 1981, ed. Jack E. Smith, (Mesa Verde, Colorado: Mesa Verde Museum Association).

LIPE, WILLIAM D.
1978   "The Southwest," in *Ancient Native Americans*, ed. Jesse D. Jennings, 403-454, (San Francisco: W. H. Freeman).

LISTER, ROBERT H.
1966   "Contributions to Mesa Verde Archaeology III: Site 866 and the Cultural Sequence at Four Villages in the Far View Group, Mesa Verde National Park, Colorado," *University of Colorado Studies, Series in Anthropology* 12, (Boulder).

LISTER, ROBERT H., AND FLORENCE C. LISTER
1977   *Earl Morris and Southwestern Archaeology* (reprint of 1968 edition), (Albuquerque: University of New Mexico Press).

1981   *Chaco Canyon: Archaeology and Archaeologists*, (Albuquerque: University of New Mexico Press).

1983   *Those Who Came Before*, Southwest Parks and Monuments Association, (Tucson: University of Arizona Press).

LONGACRE, WILLIAM A. (ED.)
1970   *Reconstructing Prehistoric Pueblo Societies*, (Albuquerque: University of New Mexico Press).

MADSEN, DAVID B., AND MICHAEL S. BERRY
1975   "A Reassessment of Northeastern Great Basin Prehistory," *American Antiquity* 40(1):82-86.

MALOTKI, EKKEHART
1978   *Hopitutuwutsi: Hopi Tales*, (Flagstaff: Museum of Northern Arizona Press).

MARSHALL, MICHAEL P., AND HENRY J. WALT
1984   *Rio Abajo: Prehistory and History of a Rio Grande Province*, (Santa Fe: New Mexico Historic Preservation Program).

MARTIN, PAUL S.
1936   "Lowry Ruin in Southwestern Colorado," *Field Museum of Natural History, Publications, Anthropological Series*, vol. 35, no. 1, (Chicago).

1979   "Prehistory: Mogollon," in *Handbook of North American Indians*, vol. 9 Southwest: 61-74, ed. Alfonso Ortiz, (Washington, D. C.: Smithsonian Institution).

MARTIN, PAUL S., AND FRED PLOG
1973   *The Archaeology of Arizona: A Study of the Southwest Region*, (Garden City, N. Y.: Doubleday and Natural History Press).

MARTIN, PAUL S., JOHN B. RINALDO, ELAINE A. BLUHM, HUGH C. CUTLER, AND ROGER GRANGE, JR.
1952   "Mogollon Cultural Continuity and Change: the Stratigraphic Analysis of Tularosa and Cordova Caves," *Fieldiana: Anthropology*, vol. 40, (Chicago: Field Museum of Natural History).

MARWITT, JOHN P.
1970   "Median Village and Fremont Culture Regional Variation," *University of Utah Anthropological Papers*, no. 95, (Salt Lake City).

MCGREGOR, JOHN C.
1967   *Southwestern Archaeology*, (Urbana: University of Illinois Press).

MCKENNA, PETER J., AND MARSHA TRUELL
1986   "Small Site Architecture of Chaco Canyon, New Mexico," *Publications in Archaeology* 18D, Chaco Canyon Studies, National Park Service, (Santa Fe).

MERA, HARRY P.
1939   "Style Trends of Pueblo Pottery in the Rio Grande and Little Colorado Cultural Area from the Sixteenth to the Nineteenth Century"

MORRIS, EARL H.
1919   "Preliminary Account of the Antiquities of the Region Between the Mancos and LaPlata Rivers in Southwestern Colorado," *Bureau of American Ethnology*, 33rd Annual Report:155-206, (Washington, D. C.: Smithsonian Institution).

1921   "The House of the Great Kiva at the Aztec Ruin," *Anthropological Papers of the American Museum of Natural History*, vol. 26, pt. 2:109-138, (New York).

1928   "Notes on Excavations in the Aztec Ruin," *Anthropological Papers of the American Museum of Natural History*, vol. 26, no. 5:259-420, (New York).

1939   "Archaeological Studies in the LaPlata District, Southwestern Colorado and Northwestern New Mexico," *Carnegie Institution of Washington, Publication* 519, (Washington, D. C.)

MORRIS, EARL H., AND ROBERT F. BURGH
1954   "Basket Maker II Sites Near Durango, Colorado," *Carnegie Institution of Washington, Publication* 604, (Washington, D. C.).

NEQUATEWA, EDMOND
1947   *The Truth of a Hopi*, (Flagstaff: Northern Arizona Society of Science and Art).

NEWCOMB, W. W., JR., AND FORREST KIRKLAND
1967   *The Rock Art of the Texas Indians*, (Austin: University of Texas Press).

NOBLE, DAVID GRANT
1981   *Ancient Ruins of the Southwest*, (Flagstaff: Northland Press).

NOBLE, DAVID GRANT (ED.)
1980   "Bandelier National Monument," *Exploration*, (Santa Fe: School of American Research).

1981   "Pecos Ruins," *Explorations*, (Santa Fe: School of American Research).

1982   "Salinas," *Explorations*, (Santa Fe: School of American Research).

1983   "Zuni El Morro: Past and Present," *Explorations*, (Santa Fe: School of American Research).

1984   *New Light on Chaco Canyon*, (Santa Fe: School of American Research Press).

1986   "Tse Yaa Kin," *Explorations*, (Santa Fe: School of American Research).

NORDENSKIÖLD, GUSTAV
1893 *The Cliff Dwellers of the Mesa Verde, Southwestern Colorado: Their Pottery and Implements*, trans. D. Lloyd Morgan, (Stockholm and Chicago), reprint 1980 (Glorieta: Rio Grande Press).

ORTIZ, ALFONSO (ED.)
1973 *The Tewa World: Space, Time, Being and Becoming in a Pueblo Society*, (Chicago: University of Chicago Press).

1972a "Ritual Drama and the Pueblo World," in *New Perspectives on the Pueblos*:135-161, (Albuquerque: University of New Mexico Press).

1972b *New Perspectives on the Pueblos*, (Albuquerque: University of New Mexico Press).

1979 *Handbook of North American Indians*, vol. 9, Southwest, (Washington, D. C.: Smithsonian Institution).

PARMENTIER, RICHARD J.
1979 "The Pueblo Mythological Triangle: Poseyemu, Montezuma, and Jesus," in *Handbook of North American Indians*, vol. 9 Southwest:609-622, ed. Alfonso Ortiz, (Washington: Smithsonian Institution).

PARSONS, ELSIE CLEWS
1936 "Introduction," in "Hopi Journal of Alexander M. Stephen" (2 vols.), ed. Elsie Clews Parsons, *Columbia University Contributions to Anthropology* 23, (New York).

1939 *Pueblo Indian Religion*, (2 vols.), (Chicago: University of Chicago Press).

PEPPER, GEORGE H.
1920 "Pueblo Bonito," *Anthropological Papers of the American Museum of Natural History*, vol. 27, (New York).

PICKERING, ROBERT B. (ED.)
1976 "Archaeological Frontiers: Papers on New World High Cultures in Honor of J. Charles Kelley," *University Museum Studies*, no. 4, (Carbondale: University Museum and Art Galleries, Southern Illinois University).

PIKE, DONALD G.
1974 *Anasazi: Ancient People of the Rock*, (New York: Crown Publishers).

PLOG, FRED
1979 "Prehistory: Western Anasazi," in *Handbook of North American Indians*, vol. 9, Southwest:108-130, ed. Alfonso Ortiz, (Washington, D. C.: Smithsonian Institution).

POWERS, ROBERT P.
1984 "Outliers and Roads in the Chaco System," in *New Light on Chaco Canyon*, ed. David Grant Noble, (Santa Fe: School of American Research).

POWERS, ROBERT P., WILLIAM B. GILLESPIE, AND STEPHEN H. LEKSON
1983 "The Outlier Survey," *Division of Cultural Research*, U. S. National Park Service, Reports of the Chaco Center, no. 3, (Albuquerque).

REED, ERIK K.
1964 "The Greater Southwest," in *Prehistoric Man in the New World*, eds. Jesse D. Jennings and Edward Norbeck, (Chicago: University of Chicago Press).

RILEY, CARROLL L.
1971 "Early Spanish-Indian Communication in the Greater Southwest," *New Mexico Historical Review*, vol. 46:285-314, (Albuquerque: University of New Mexico).

1975 "Pueblo Indians in Meso-America: the Early Historic Period," in "Collected Papers in Honor of Florence Hawley Ellis":454-462, ed. Theodore Frisbie, *Papers of the Archaeological Society of New Mexico*, no. 2, (Norman: Hooper Publishing Co.).

1978 "Pecos and Trade," in *Across the Chichimec Sea: Essays in Honor of J. Charles Kelley*:53-64, eds. Carroll L. Riley and Basil C. Hedrick, (Carbondale: Southern Illinois University).

RILEY, CARROLL L., AND BASIL C. HEDRICK (EDS.)
1978 *Across the Chichimec Sea: Essays in Honor of J. Charles Kelley*, (Carbondale: Southern Illinois University).

ROBERTS, FRANK H. H., JR.
1931 "The Ruins of Kiatuthlanna, Eastern Arizona," *Bureau of American Ethnology, Bulletin* 100, (Washington, D. C.).

1932 "The Village of the Great Kivas on the Zuni Reservation, New Mexico," *Bureau of American Ethnology, Bulletin* 111, (Washington, D. C.)

1935 "A Survey of Southwestern Archaeology," *American Anthropologist*, vol. 37:1-33.

ROHN, ARTHUR H.
1971 "Mug House, Mesa Verde National Park, Colorado," *National Park Service, Archaeological Research Series* 7-D, (Washington, D. C.)

SAHAGÚN, BERNARDINO DE
1959 *Florentine Codex: General History of the Things of New Spain. Book 9, the Merchants*, eds. and trans. A. J. O. Anderson and Charles E. Dibble, (Santa Fe: University of Utah and School of American Research).

SANDO, JOE S.
1982 *Nee Hemish: A History of Jemez Pueblo*, (Albuquerque: University of New Mexico Press).

SAYLES, E. B., AND A. ANTEVS
1941 "The Cochise Culture," *Medallion Papers* 29, (Globe, Arizona: Gila Pueblo).

SCHAAFSMA, POLLY
1971 "The Rock Art of Utah," *Papers of the Peabody Museum of American Archaeology and Ethnology*, vol. 65, (Cambridge: Harvard University).

1972 *Rock Art of New Mexico*, (Santa Fe: State Planning Office).

1980 *Indian Rock Art of the Southwest*, (Albuquerque: School of American Research and University of New Mexico Press).

SCHAAFSMA, POLLY, AND CURTIS F. SCHAAFSMA
1974 "Evidence for the Origins of the Pueblo Kachina Cult as Suggested by Southwestern Rock Art," *American Antiquity*, vol. 39:535-545.

SCHROEDER, ALBERT H.
1960 "The Hohokam, Sinagua, and Hakataya," *Society for American Archaeology, Archives of Archaeology* 5.

1972 "Rio Grande Ethnohistory," in *New Perspectives on the Pueblos*, ed. Alfonso Ortiz, (Albuquerque: School of American Research and University of New Mexico Press).

1979 "Pueblos Abandoned in Historic Times," in *Handbook of North American Indians*, vol. 9, Southwest:236-254, ed. Alfonso Ortiz, (Washington, D. C.: Smithsonian Institution).

SCHROEDL, ALAN R.
1977 "The Grand Canyon Figurine Complex," *American Antiquity*, vol. 42:254-265.

SIMMONS, MARC
1979 "History of Pueblo-Spanish Relations to 1821," in *Handbook of North American Indians*, vol. 9, Southwest:178-193, ed. Alfonso Ortiz, (Washington, D. C.: Smithsonian Institution).

SIMMONS, ALAN H. (ED.)
1982 "Prehistoric Adaptive Strategies in the Chaco Canyon Region, Northwestern New Mexico. Vol. 2: Site Reports," *Navajo Nation Papers in Anthropology*, no. 9, (Window Rock: Navajo Nation Cultural Resource Management Program).

SIMPSON, T. JAMES H.
1852 *Journal of a Military Reconnaissance from Santa Fe, New Mexico, to the Navajo Country*, (Philadelphia: Lippincott, Grambo and Co.).

SMITH, WATSON
1952 "Kiva Mural Decorations at Awatovi and Kawaika-a, with a Survey of other Wall Paintings in the Pueblo Southwest," *Papers of the Peabody Museum of*

American Archaeology and Ethnology, vol. 37, (Cambridge: Harvard University).

SOFAER, ANNA, VOLKER ZINSER, AND ROLF SINCLAIR
1979   "A Unique Solar Marking Construct," *Science*, 206.

SPICER, EDWARD H.
1962   *Cycles of Conquest*, (Tucson: University of Arizona Press).

STEPHEN, ALEXANDER M.
1936   "Hopi Journal of Alexander M. Stephen," ed. Elsie Clews Parson, 2 vols., *Columbia University, Contributions to Anthropology*, vol. 23, (New York).

STEVENSON, MATILDA COXE
1894   "The Sia," *Bureau of American Ethnology,* 11th Annual Report for the Years 1889-1890, (Washington, D. C.: Smithsonian Institution).
1904   "The Zuni Indians," *Bureau of American Ethnology,* 23rd Annual Report for the Years 1901-1902, (Washington, D. C.: Smithsonian Institution).

STIRLING, MATTHEW W.
1942   "Origin Myth of Acoma and Other Records," *Bureau of American Ethnology Bulletin* 135, (Washington, D. C.: Smithsonian Institution).

STUART, DAVID E., AND RORY GAUTHIER
1981   *Prehistoric New Mexico*, (Santa Fe: New Mexico Historic Preservation Bureau).

TANNER, CLARA LEE
1976   *Prehistoric Southwestern Craft Arts*, (Tucson: University of Arizona Press).

TEDLOCK, DENNIS
1979   "Zuni Religion and World View," in *Handbook of North American Indians,* vol. 9, Southwest:499-508, ed. Alfonso Ortiz, (Washington, D. C.: Smithsonian Institution).

TEDLOCK, DENNIS (TRANS.)
1972   *Finding the Center: Narrative Poetry of the Zuni Indians, from Performances in Zuni,* by Andrew Peynetsa and Walter Sanchez, (New York: Dial Press).

TOLL, H. WOLCOTT
1984   "Trends in Ceramic Import and Distribution in Chaco Canyon," in *Recent Research on Chaco Prehistory, Reports of the Chaco Center* no. 8:115-135, eds. W. James Judge and John D. Schelberg, (Albuquerque: National Park Service.)

UNDERHILL, RUTH M.
1965   *Red Man's Religion*, (Chicago: University of Chicago Press).

VIVIAN, R. GORDON
1935a   "Frescoes Uncovered at Kuaua," *El Palacio*, vol. 38, nos. 9, 10, 11:61, (Santa Fe).
1935b   "The Murals at Kuaua," *El Palacio*, vol. 38, nos. 21, 22, 23:113-119, (Santa Fe).

VIVIAN, R. GORDON, AND PAUL REITER
1960   "The Great Kivas of Chaco Canyon and Their Relationships," *Monographs of the School of American Research* 22, (Santa Fe).

VIVIAN, R. GWINN
1970   "An Inquiry Into Prehistoric Social Organization in Chaco Canyon, New Mexico," in *Reconstructing Prehistoric Pueblo Societies*:59-83, ed. William A. Longacre, (Albuquerque: University of New Mexico Press).

VIVIAN, R. GWINN, DULCE N. DODGEN, AND GAYLE H. HARTMAN
1978   "Wooden Ritual Artifacts from Chaco Canyon, New Mexico," *Anthropological Papers of the University of Arizona*, no. 32, (Tucson: University of Arizona Press).

WEAVER, DONALD E., JR.
1984   *Images on Stone: The Prehistoric Rock Art of the Colorado Plateau*, (Flagstaff: Museum of Northern Arizona).

WENDORF, FRED, AND ERIK K. REED
1955   "An Alternative Reconstruction of Northern Rio Grande Prehistory," *El Palacio*, vol. 62, nos. 5, 6:131-173.

WHITE, LESLIE A.
1932a   "The Pueblo of San Felipe," *American Anthropological Association, Memoirs,* no. 38:1 - 69, (Menasha, Wisc.).
1932b   "The Acoma Indians," *Bureau of American Ethnology,* 47th Annual Report for the Years 1929-1930:17-192, (Washington, D. C.: Smithsonian Institution).
1935   "The Pueblo of Santo Domingo, New Mexico," *American Anthropological Association Memoirs*, no. 43:1-210, (Menasha, Wisc.).
1942   "The Pueblo of Santa Ana, New Mexico," *American Anthropological Association Memoirs,* no. 60:1-360, (Menasha, Wisc.)
1962   "The Pueblo of Sia, New Mexico," *Bureau of American Ethnology Bulletin* 184, (Washington, D. C.: Smithsonian Institution).

WILLEY, GORDON R.
1966   *An Introduction to American Archaeology,* vol. 1: North and Middle America (Englewood Cliffs, N. J.: Prentice-Hall).

WILLEY, GORDON R., AND JEREMY A. SABLOFF
1980   *A History of American Archaeology*, (San Francisco: W. H. Freeman and Co.).

WILLIAMS, JERRY L. (ED.)
1986   *New Mexico in Maps*, (Albuquerque: University of New Mexico Press).

WILLIAMSON, RAY A.
1984   *Living the Sky*, (Boston: Houghton Mifflin Co.).

WOODBURY, RICHARD B.
1956   "The Antecedents of Zuni Culture," *Transactions of the New York Academy of Sciences*, 2d. series, vol. 18, no. 6:557-563, (New York).

WOODBURY, RICHARD B.
1979   "Prehistory: Introduction," in *Handbook of North American Indians,* vol. 9 Southwest:22-30, ed. Alfonso Ortiz, (Washington, D. C.: Smithsonian Institution).

WOODBURY, RICHARD B., AND EZRA B. W. ZUBROW
1979   "Agricultural Beginnings, 2000 B.C.-A.D. 500," in *Handbook of North American Indians,* vol. 9, Southwest:43-60, ed. Alfonso Ortiz, (Washington, D. C.: Smithsonian Institution).

YAVA, ALBERT
1978   *Big Falling Snow: A Tewa-Hopi Indian's Life and Times and the History and Traditions of His People,* ed. and annot. Harold Courlander, (Albuquerque: University of New Mexico Press).

List of Plates

34. *Pit house at Chaco Canyon, northwestern New Mexico.*

35. *Two gourd-shaped pottery ladles, Kayenta tradition. Laboratory of Anthropology, Museum of New Mexico, Santa Fe.*

36. *Pottery Bowl, Cibola/Chaco tradition. Laboratory of Anthropology, Museum of New Mexico, Santa Fe.*

37. *Wrapped weave sandals. San Juan region. Laboratory of Anthropology, Museum of New Mexico, Santa Fe.*

38. *Carrying bag. Southern Utah. Laboratory of Anthropology, Museum of New Mexico, Santa Fe.*

39. *Habitation site at a rock shelter, Natural Bridges, southeastern Utah.*

40. *Waterfall run-off from the mesa-top following a summer shower, Chaco Canyon, New Mexico.*

41. *Check dams and agricultural terraces, Gila Mountains, New Mexico. ca. eleventh century.*

42. *Kiva, Twin Trees Site 102, Mesa Verde.*

43. *Deep pit house, Twin Trees Site 103.*

44. *Kiva, Ruins Road Site 16, Mesa Verde, Colorado.*

45. *Coombs Village, Kayenta district, southern Utah (Reconstructed.)*

46. *Jacal wall of a room in a rock shelter at Grand Gulch, southeastern Utah, Mesa Verde-Kayenta borderlands.*

47. *Red Mesa black-on-white jar. Laboratory of Anthropology, Museum of New Mexico, Santa Fe.*

48. *Bowl and canteen, Cibola/Chaco mineral-paint tradition. Laboratory of Anthropology, Museum of New Mexico, Santa Fe.*

49. *Double bowl, Cibola/Chaco mineral-painted tradition. Laboratory of Anthropology, Museum of New Mexico, Santa Fe.*

50. *Bowl from Chaco Canyon; Mesa Verde bowl; seed jar from the Kayenta region. Laboratory of Anthropology, Museum of New Mexico, Santa Fe.*

51. *Mesa Verde-style carbon-paint bowl. Laboratory of Anthropology, Museum of New Mexico, Santa Fe.*

52. *Shell necklace and two pendants. Laboratory of Anthropology, Museum of New Mexico, Santa Fe.*

53. *Carved slate paint palette, turtle effigy stone bowl, stone arrowhead, and clay figurine fragment. Maxwell Museum of Anthropology, Albuquerque.*

54. *Aerial view of Chaco Canyon looking southwest, New Mexico.*

55. *The Tower Kiva of Chetro Ketl, Chaco Canyon.*

56. *Overview of Cliff Palace, Mesa Verde, Colorado.*

57. *Cliff Palace, Mesa Verde.*

58. *Overview of Antelope House, Canyon de Chelly, Kayenta District, Arizona.*

59. *Antelope House, Canyon de Chelly.*

60. *An ancient wooden ceiling preserved at Pueblo Bonito, Chaco Canyon, northwestern New Mexico.*

61. *Interior of Pueblo del Arroyo, Chaco Canyon.*

62. 63. *Doorways within Pueblo Bonito, Chaco Canyon.*

64. *Milling basins for grinding corn, in a rock shelter in Grand Gulch, southeastern Utah.*

65. *Wooden hoes and digging sticks. National Park Service, Chaco Canyon.*

66. *Coiled basket of natural fibers. Cibola region. Chamber of Commerce Museum, Grants, New Mexico.*

67. *Pueblo Bonito from the air, looking north. Chaco Canyon, New Mexico.*

68. 69. *Great Kiva and kiva, Pueblo Bonito.*

70. *Overview of Pueblo Bonito.*

71. *A suite of ground floor rooms of Pueblo Bonito at Chaco Canyon.*

72. 73. *Great Kiva of Casa Rinconada at Chaco Canyon.*

74. *An alley-like ground-floor passageway at Chetro Ketl, Chaco Canyon.*

75. *Tower kiva and signalling station at the Chaco outlier called Kin Ya'a, New Mexico.*

76. *Fajada Butte looms over the south entrance to Chaco Canyon in the early morning mist.*

77. *The so-called Sun-Dagger petroglyph atop Fajada Butte in May, 1985.*

78. *Chacoan Great Kiva at the large Chaco outlier called Aztec, northwestern New Mexico. (Reconstructed.)*

79. *Great Kiva, Aztec, inside view.*

80. *Great Kiva, Aztec. Access to one of the fourteen small rooms encircling the kiva.*

81. *Shell and jet necklaces and many pieces of worked turquoise found in the Great Kiva at Chetro Ketl, Chaco Canyon. School of American Research Collections at the Museum of New Mexico, Santa Fe.*

82. 83. *Gallup olla. Laboratory of Anthropology, Museum of New Mexico, Santa Fe.*

84. *A basketry tube, a bone instrument, and a drinking mug recovered at Pueblo Bonito, Chaco Canyon. American Museum of Natural History, New York.*

85. *Three pottery vessels recovered from excavations at Chaco Canyon: boot-shaped jar with animal handle, bird-shaped jar, gourd-shaped ladle. School of American Research Collection at the Museum of New Mexico, Santa Fe.*

86. *Cliff Palace, Mesa Verde, Colorado.*

87. *Dance plaza with kiva hidden within it at Cliff Palace, Mesa Verde.*

88. *Cliff Palace, Mesa Verde. Monochromatic painting high up in a tower.*

89. *Cliff Palace, Mesa Verde.*

90. *Far View House, at Mesa Verde.*

91. *Sun Temple at Mesa Verde.*

92. *Far View Tower at Mesa Verde.*

93. 94. *Small kivas at Far View House, Mesa Verde.*

95. *Kiva at Far View House, Mesa Verde.*

96. *Sun Temple, Mesa Verde.*

97. *Kiva at Lowry Ruin, a Chaco outlier west and north of Mesa Verde.*

98. *Betatakin, a western Kayenta village in Tsegi Canyon, northern Arizona.*

99. *Antelope House Ruin, Canyon de Chelly, eastern Kayenta District, Arizona.*

100. *Mesa Verde and Kayenta pottery: canteen, ladle, mug, and bowl. Indian Art Fund, School of American Research, Santa Fe.*

101. 102. *Two views of the White House Ruin, Canyon de Chelly eastern Kayenta District, Arizona.*

103. *Wupatki, a Sinagua site built near Sunset Crater in northern Arizona.*

104. *Pottery bowl, Mimbres, southwestern New Mexico. Maxwell Museum of Anthropology, Albuquerque.*

105. *Pottery bowl, St. John's polychrome, west-central New Mexico and east-central Arizona. Laboratory of Anthropology, Museum of New Mexico, Santa Fe.*

106. *Montezuma Castle, a Sinagua site in the Verde Valley below the Mogollon Rim, north-central Arizona.*

107. *Rock engraving from Cerro de los Indios, middle Rio Grande Valley.*

108. *Ornaments of shell, turquoise, and Arizona pipestone. Laboratory of Anthropology, Museum of New Mexico, Santa Fe.*

109. *Pottery jar, Pajarito Plateau, northern Rio Grande. Indian Art Fund, School of American Research, Santa Fe.*

110. *Two glaze polychrome pottery bowls. Indian Art Fund, School of American Research, Santa Fe.*

111. *Pottery bowl, glaze polychrome, middle Rio Grande Valley. Maxwell Museum of Anthropology, Albuquerque.*

112. *Painted kiva at the site of Kuaua, Rio Grande Valley, New Mexico. (Replica.)*

113. *Engraved rock picture of a masked hunter and a large crane at the site of Cerro de los Indios, New Mexico.*

114. *Painted kachina images in a shallow rock shelter near the Salinas Pueblo of Tenebo, New Mexico.*

115. *Two pottery bowls and canteen, Rio Grande district. Laboratory of Anthropology, Museum of New Mexico, Santa Fe.*

116. *Selenite pendants, Rio Grande. Laboratory of Anthropology, Museum of New Mexico, Santa Fe.*

117. *Tyonyi in Frijoles Canyon, Pajarito Plateau, New Mexico.*

118. 119. *Tsankawi on the Pajarito Plateau, New Mexico.*

120. *Ruins of the Spanish mission at Gran Quivira, New Mexico.*

121. *Sapawe in the Chama River Valley, adjacent to the Pajarito Plateau, northern Rio Grande district, New Mexico.*

122. *The Stone Lion shrine on the Pajarito Plateau, New Mexico.*

List of Illustrations in Text

37. Rio Grande canteen, northern New Mexico. Maxwell Museum of Anthropology, Albuquerque.

38. Hohokam pottery bowl with dancing figures. Laboratory of Anthropology, Museum of New Mexico, Santa Fe.

39. Hohokam engraved rock art with standing figures. Original in Tucson Basin.

40. Fremont style rock art, petroglyphs. Fruita Point, Capitol Reef, southern Utah.

41. The Anasazi world during the Classic period.

42. "Restoration of the Pueblo Hungo Pavie (Crooked Nose)." Lithograph after a watercolor by Richard H. Kern, 1849.

43. Houses and storerooms in a rock crevice within a rock shelter, Grand Gulch, southeastern Utah.

44. A wooden ceiling in a room at Spruce Tree House, Mesa Verde, Colorado.

45. Large timbers placed as stringers within the walls at Chetro Ketl in Chaco Canyon, New Mexico.

46. Maize-grinding room with *metates* and *manos* set side-by-side, Mesa Verde.

47. Fragment of reversed twill tapestry loom-woven cotton fabric from Grand Gulch, Utah. University Museum, University of Pennsylvania.

48. The San Juan Basin, Chaco Canyon and the Chaco system of roads and outlying communities.

49. Guadalupe Ruin, a Chaco outlier along the Rio Puerco, east of Chaco Canyon.

50. The site of Grey Hills, a Chaco outlier.

51. Simplified plan views of some Chaco Great Houses.

52. The Chaco method for building large, multi-storied houses.

53. Painting by Lloyd Townsend of Pueblo Bonito at Chaco Canyon as it was in about 1100.

54. Construction sequence at Pueblo Bonito.

55. Sandstone disks, Great Kiva at Chetro Ketl.

56. Landscapes that surround a Pueblo community and the kivas built within them are metaphors for the structured universe.

57. Plan of eleventh-century garden plots ("waffle gardens") and irrigation system near Chetro Ketl.

58. Jackson Staircase, behind Chetro Ketl.

59. The so-called Sun-Dagger atop Fajada Butte marked both solstices and equinoxes.

60. Petroglyphs behind the Great House called Kin Kletso at Chaco Canyon.

61. Spiral and water animals, rock art of the Cibola District. Originals at the Village of the Great Kivas, a Chaco outlier near modern Zuni Pueblo in northwestern New Mexico.

62. A fragment of a painted wooden ritual object from the Chaco Canyon site of Chetro Ketl. National Park Service.

63. The remains of a Mexican macaw that was ritually buried at the Chaco outlier called Salmon Ruin.

64. Chaco effigy vessel, fragment. From Pueblo Bonito. American Museum of Natural History, New York.

65. Mesa Verde canteen from Pueblo Bonito in Chaco Canyon. School of American Research Collections at the Museum of New Mexico, Santa Fe.

66. Inaccessible House, Mesa Verde.

67. The Far View Community at Mesa Verde.

68. Kiva, Far View House, Mesa Verde.

69. Cliff Palace, Mesa Verde.

70. Yellow Jacket in the Montezuma Valley, Colorado.

71. Tower structures built on top of huge boulders in Hovenweep Canyon.

72. Rook Tower at Hovenweep on the western margin of the Mesa Verde district.

73. Mesa Verde-style petroglyphs, Grand Gulch, southeastern Utah.

74. Pottery bowl, Mesa Verde black-on-white. University Museum, University of Pennsylvania.

75. Split Level Ruin, Grand Gulch, southeastern Utah.

76. White House Ruins in Canyon de Chelly, Arizona.

77. Antelope House, detail. Canyon de Chelly, Arizona.

78. Kayenta pictographs from the site of Betatakin.

79. Black painted cotton textile from Hidden House, central Arizona.

80. Kayenta-style pottery bowl from northern Arizona.

Laboratory of Anthropology, Museum of New Mexico, Santa Fe.

81. Kayenta-style pottery bowl from Betatakin at the northern end of Black Mesa. Indian Art Fund, School of American Research.

82. Pottery bowl from the White Mountain area of east-central Arizona. Laboratory of Anthropology, Museum of New Mexico, Santa Fe.

83. Reconstruction of the Galaz site in the Mimbres Valley.

84. Pottery jar, Jemez Mountains district, New Mexico. Indian Art Fund, School of American Research.

85.86. Two pottery bowls, Sikyatki polychrome, Hopi Pueblos. University Museum, University of Pennsylvania.

87. Hopi shrine with clan symbols at Willow Springs near the Grand Canyon, Arizona.

88. Petroglyphs of kachina masks at Cerro de los Indios on the Rio Grande in central New Mexico.

89. Probable migration routes leading to the Pueblo IV settlements at the time of the Spanish invasions.

90. Taos Pueblo, model by William Henry Jackson, 1877. Museum of New Mexico, Santa Fe.

91. Acoma Pueblo, aerial view.

92. Petroglyph of a warrior, almost life-size, Comanche Gap, Galisteo Basin, north-central New Mexico.

93. Wall paintings inside a small cave at Cerro de los Indios, Rio Grande Valley, central New Mexico.

94. Petroglyphs near Pueblo Blanco, Galisteo Basin, north-central New Mexico.

95. Acoma Pueblo.

96. Zuni Pueblo, Halona, from the Zuni River.

97. The Hopi Pueblo of Oraibi.

98. Peach trees, beans, corn, and chilies grow in the sand dunes near the modern Hopi pueblos in northeastern Arizona.

99. Serigraph copy by Louie Ewing of a kiva mural from the Hopi town of Awatovi.

100. Pottery bowl, Zuni Pueblo, Ashiwi polychrome. Indian Art Fund, School of American Research.

101. Wall painting on the east wall of the Franciscan mission church at the Jemez Pueblo of Guisewa.

Index

Numbers in italics refer to the illustrations:
plate numbers are followed by *Pl.*
and illustrations for the text by *ill.*

Illustration Credits

Plates

Tom Baker: 31, 54, 67, 121. J. J. Brody: 23, 24, 26, 27, 28, 29, 30, 32, 33, 40, 41, 42, 43, 44, 45, 46, 57, 63, 72, 87, 88, 89, 93, 94, 98, 103, 106, 107, 112, 113, 117, 118, 119, 122. Alberto Contri: 3, 5, 6, 58, 59, 99, 101, 102. Deborah Flynn: 66, 84. Rodney Hook: 9, 10, 11, 12, 13, 14, 15, 16, 17, 18, 19, 20, 21, 22, 35, 36, 37, 38, 47, 48, 49, 50, 51, 52, 53, 65, 81, 82, 83, 85, 100, 104, 105, 108, 109, 110, 111, 115, 116. Editoriale Jaca Book (photo Giovanna Belcastro and Enrico Noli): 56, 68, 69, 70, 78, 79, 80, 86, 90, 91, 92, 95, 96. Dudley W. King: 4, 7, 8, 25, 39, 55, 61, 62, 64, 71, 73, 74, 97, 114, 120. Kim McLean: 60, 75, 76. National Park Service and Maxwell Museum of Anthropology: 34, 77. Gianni Perotti: 1, 2.

Illustrations in Text

Photographs

American Museum of Natural History: 22. J. J. Brody: 30, 43, 47, 49, 71, 74, 85, 86, 93, 98. Alberto Contri: 77. Rodney Hook: 6, 14, 23, 29, 33, 36, 37, 38, 65, 80, 81, 82, 84, 100. Editoriale Jaca Book (photo Giovanna Belcastro and Enrico Noli): 46, 55, 68. Dudley W. King: 2, 3, 18, 72, 75. Maxwell Museum of Anthropology: 16, 62, 64. Museum of New Mexico: 7, 31, 44, 45, 58, 66, 69, 76, 90, 91, 95, 96, 97, 101. National Park Service and Maxwell Museum of Anthropology: 50, 53, 63. David Noble: 12. School of American Research Collections at the Museum of New Mexico: 15. Don Weaver: 87.

Line Drawings

Editoriale Jaca Book (Maria Jorrin): 28; (Katrina Lasko): 1, 4, 5, 11, 17, 19, 20, 21, 24, 25, 26, 27, 32, 34, 35, 39, 40, 41, 48, 51, 52, 54, 56, 57, 59, 60, 61, 67, 70, 73, 78, 79, 83, 88, 89, 92, 94.